Published by
The Liffey Press
Ashbrook House, 10 Main Street
Raheny, Dublin 5, Ireland
www.theliffeypress.com

© 2013 Stephen J. Costello

A catalogue record of this book is
available from the British Library.

ISBN 978-1-908308-46-7

Printed in Ireland by SPRINT-print Ltd.

THE TRUTH ABOUT LYING

With Some Differences Between Men and Women

Stephen J. Costello

The Liffey Press

About the Author

Stephen J. Costello, Ph.D., is a philosopher and Director of the Viktor Frankl Institute of Ireland: School of Logotherapy and Existential Analysis. He was born in Dublin and educated in St. Gerard's School, Castleknock College, University College Dublin and did a small stint at the King's Inns. He holds a Master's and doctorate degree in philosophy from the National University of Ireland and a Diploma in Logotherapy and Existential Analysis from Vienna. Dr Costello is the author of *The Irish Soul: In Dialogue, The Pale Criminal: Psychoanalytic Perspectives, 18 Reasons Why Mothers Hate Their Babies: A Philosophy of Childhood, Hermeneutics and the Psychoanalysis of Religion, What are Friends For?: Insights from the Great Philosophers, The Ethics of Happiness: An Existential Analysis,* and *Philosophy and the Flow of Presence: Desire, Drama and the Divine Ground of Being.* Dr Costello is a member of the Irish Philosophical Society, the Royal Institute of Philosophy and the International Association of Logotherapy and Existential Analysis. He is a black belt in Aikido and the equivalent in Wing Tsun Kung Fu.

Contents

I dedicate this book to Darren –
the friend I don't deserve to have.

Acknowledgements

I mention only those who have directly contributed to the writing of this book by way of reading earlier drafts, advising, suggesting titles or commenting constructively. To this end, I extend my heartfelt thanks to my very patient friends: Fionnuala Mac-Aodha, Shay Ward, Oisín Breathnach, the Kearney brothers, Aedamar Kirrane, Cathal O'Keeffe, Michael Fitzpatrick, Bob Haugh, Helen Sheehan, William Corrigan, and John Rice, *in memoriam*. This list includes my parents too, so special thanks to Val and Johnny Costello, who have always been there for me.

For providing such a gratifying paragraph of praise and for the equally ambrosial Foreword I extend my inestimable appreciation to Professors Richard Kearney and Ivor Browne, who have done me some service, merited or not. I am deeply honoured.

Finally, a profuse and profound debt of gratitude goes to my closest friend, Darren Cleary, to whom I dedicate this book. You inspire and ennoble me, enhance and enrich my life in more ways than you will ever know, for which I thank you from the bottom of my heart. You are a stalwart pillar of support and this book is all the better for your perusal.

Foreword

This is an absolutely fascinating book, and perhaps what is more important, a most enjoyable one to read. Stephen Costello is a serious philosopher and highly trained psychotherapist with enormous erudition. One would hardly need to refer to Google if you could call on his personal services. He has, at his fingertips, an extraordinary range of literary and philosophical sources and he can call on these apparently without effort.

At the same time he draws the reader into a personal dialogue in a simple and intimate way, and there is a subtle thread of humour running through the whole book that makes reading it all the more attractive and makes some of the more difficult passages, like the section on the philosophical views of Sartre – that, in his opinion, truth is virtually impossible to discern – more accessible to the ordinary reader like myself.

On first reading the title and opening the book, my feeling was, 'Of course I know the difference between "truth" and "lies",' but as one reads on, you realise how wrong you are, and that it is virtually impossible to discern intellectually when one is being really truthful, or engaging, as we all do, in distortions and lies of many kinds.

Then when I came to the section 'Do animals lie?' I thought, 'At least here, it's quite clear that animals are incapable of lying.' But, once again, as you continue, you realise that nature is full of deceit, and that creatures of all kinds make themselves appear bigger, stronger and quite fierce looking in order to ward off predators, and so on.

Central to the whole book is the section towards the end on 'Some Differences between Men and Women'; and this leads on to the description of 'How Men and Women Lie in Different Ways'. Here Stephen brings to bear on his subject a quite extraordinary range of information, and I can't think, for the life of me, from where he derived all of these insights.

As I said at the beginning, this is a truly fascinating book, which I feel should be mandatory reading for all of us. I can only encourage everyone to read it and thoroughly enjoy it as I did.

Professor Ivor Browne
Consultant Psychiatrist
September 2013

'Lying is a language game that needs to be learned like any other.' – *Ludwig Wittgenstein, Austrian philosopher*

'There is no truth that, in passing through awareness, does not lie.' – *Jacques Lacan, French psychoanalyst*

'Those who are able to see beyond the shadows and lies of their culture will never be understood, let alone believed, by the masses.' – *Plato, Greek philosopher*

'Oh, what a tangled web we weave
When first we practice to deceive.'
– *Sir Walter Scott, Scottish novelist and poet*

'When my love swears that she is made of truth,
I do believe her, though I know she lies ...
Therefore I lie with her and she with me,
And in our faults by lies we flatter'd be.'
– *William Shakespeare, English playwright*

Preface

A few years ago a friend phoned me to relate the following incident: 'Stephen, you won't believe what happened. It's right down your street. I was lying in bed last night beside a girl, just after, you know... Anyway, the phone rang. It was my girlfriend! She asked me what I was doing. I said, "Just lying in bed." Talk about a Freudian slip!' Indeed. He was telling the truth while lying in bed...

This book is on the philosophy and psychoanalysis of lying, and especially how men and women lie in different ways. It's about lies, love, language and logic. It's also about desire and deception, especially in our love relationships and in our loving-friendships.

How many lies do we tell? Can animals lie? Is deception detectable? Can psychotics lie? When do children start to lie? Why do we lie to ourselves? Do we need to lie? What about the people who enjoy lying? Above all, how do men and women lie differently? These are some of the questions I hope to answer.

Drawing on philosophical and Lacanian psychoanalytical insights, I am going to tell you the truth about lies.

A lie distracts, detracts from the truth. You lie if you don't want people to become aware of the truth. Total truth – who would want it? – is problematic. We are at home with lies. Lies can take place around the locus of the other person's desire or one's own ego. Some people like to be lied to; others need to be lied to. There is a difference between how men and women lie and to what end; this is centrally what the book is about, after certain other topics are also addressed.

When do we lie? Why do we lie? How do we lie? These questions will guide our applied enquiry and will be the subject matter of this brief book. In *The Magic Lantern*, Ingmar Bergman, the famous Swedish film-director, observed: 'Sometimes I have to console myself with the fact that he who has lived a lie loves the truth.' Achilles, the truth-sayer, and Odysseus, the liar, abide in us all.

We lie best in front of potential partners or to close business deals. We show off with stories. Not quite a lie, then, just a slight embellishment ... and so it begins. You can't have a completely truthful conversation with friends, parents or lovers. Isn't there always something that is kept secret, that isn't shown, that can't be said or spoken? Isn't intimacy based not only on what we share with, but on what keep from, each other? We lie (or don't tell the truth) for different reasons, to different people in different ways, for different reasons.

If truth-telling is sometimes harmful, is it true that we harm ourselves when we lie? Michel de Montaigne, the French philosopher, thought so: 'I do myself a greater injury in lying than I do to him of whom I tell a lie.' And Ralph Waldo Emerson, the American philosopher, writes similarly: 'Every violation of truth is not only a sort of suicide in the liar, but is a stab at the health of human society.' A private lie can have public consequences. But Graham Greene, the British novelist, was more realistic: 'In human relationships, kindness and lies are worth a thousand truths.' Lies of kindness, so.

If the truth is simple, it does not follow that it is easy to tell the truth. It may follow that it is difficult to lie well. Lying can be complicated. Samuel Butler, the English novelist, put it thus: 'Any fool can tell the truth, but it requires a man of some sense to know how to lie well.' Lying can be learnt. It is a language-game like any other after all. It takes practice.

What follows are some observations on the act and art of lying – a breviary of sorts. This type of terse writing has been present in the history of ideas from philosophers such as Heraclitus in the fifth-century BC to Theodor Adorno in the twentieth-century AD, which doesn't mean it works. Still, I'm optimistic.

I hope, dear reader, that you will resonate with these reflections and remarks and that they succeed in shedding some light on the sometimes sad human scene. Lies are essential to humanity and perhaps as important as the pursuit of pleasure, profit or purpose. For we are liars, all. Some people, of course, are better at it than others.

This book may be read as a companion volume to my *18 Reasons Why Mothers Hate Their Babies: A Philosophy of Childhood.* This present work is a type of manual, a compendium of sorts, a pithy primer on lying; in it I try to develop and defend a certain thesis: that men lie in the guise of truth and that women tell the truth in the guise of a lie. This requires a lot of unpacking, and of course, I am speaking generally; there are exceptions to this 'rule'. So let us begin the unravelling of this intriguing topic, for none of us is immune from lying (except perhaps the figure of the saint) and so it concerns us all. As Friedrich Nietzsche, the German philosopher, noted: lying is a condition of life. We lie to live.

If to quote is to pray ('the Bible says ...'), to write is to die (the authorial absence). So I cite a quotation from the twentieth-century Austrian philosopher Ludwig Wittgenstein, which I am fond of, by way of concluding this preface:

'I was sitting with a philosopher in the garden. He says again and again, "I know that's a tree," pointing to a tree that is near to us. Someone else arrives and hears this, and I tell them: "This fellow isn't insane. We are only doing philosophy.'"

That's all I'm doing too.

What's in a Name, Pinocchio?

We usually associate the name of Pinocchio with lying. Pinocchio was the chief protagonist in Carlo Collodi's 1883 children's classic, *The Adventures of Pinocchio*. Carved by a woodcutter called Geppetto in a small Italian village, Pinocchio was created as a wooden puppet who dreamed of becoming a real boy, which is exactly what happens in the story. However, every time this now animated puppet lies his short nose becomes longer under stress. This is his punishment for fabricating stories – his nose continues to grow until it can scarcely fit through the door.

Similarly, in real life, when a person lies they experience the 'Pinocchio Effect', which is an increase in the temperature around the nose and in the orbital muscle in the inner corner of the eye. According to a study conducted in the Department of Experimental Psychology in the University of Granada, face temperature changes when a mental effort is being made such as lying (thermography).

The 'Pinocchio Syndrome' is related to 'gelotophobia', which is a fear of being laughed at. When such people who suffer from this malady think they are being ridiculed the pattern in their body movements changes to exhibit the awkward wooden movements resembling those of wooden puppets.

And, finally, the 'Pinocchio Paradox' is a version of the liar paradox, which we will meet with later and arises when Pinocchio says: 'My nose grows now.' I won't saddle with you with the torturous logic involved but present you with the conclusion: his nose is growing if and only if it is not growing. Get it? No, me neither.

Definitions

Philosophers love beginning with definitions so let's define a lie in terms of the proverbial dictionary definition: 1) A lie is a type of deception in the form of an untruthful statement, especially with the intention of deceiving others. 2) A lie is a false statement made with deliberate attempt to deceive. However, St. Thomas Aquinas, the mediaeval philosopher-theologian, defines lying as a statement that is at variance with the mind. This is phrased differently to the usual definitions on the subject. It is not a false statement made with the intention of deceiving because it is possible to lie without making a false statement and without any intention of deceiving. For if a person makes a statement which he or she thinks is false, but which in reality is true, he certainly lies in as much as he intends to say what is false, and although a well-known liar may have no intention of deceiving others (for he knows that no one believes a word he says), yet if he speaks at variance with his mind he does not cease to lie. 'Sophistry' may be defined as the deliberate desire to deceive. Let's explore this subject more thoroughly.

Such Sophistry:
Philosophical Beginnings

For Aristotle, 'all men by nature desire to know', but the world seems intent on hiding itself from prying, philosophical eyes. Likewise, in the epic poems of Homer there is the view expressed that the world resists attempts to penetrate its secret mysteries. It is obdurate to every effort to understand it. Homer's poems depict a world that is replete with ruses and semblance, swindles and sham, fictions and fallacies, artifice and allure, so much so that it seems that cheating rather than plain dealing (or Freemasonic square-dealing) is the only way to advance. Odysseus hid his true identity from Athene while Athene herself was renowned for her plots and disguises and acts of dissimulation and deviousness. Hermes, the trickster god, is likewise linked to cunning communication; he uses words to veil and inveigle. Do any of us say what we really mean? Language conceals as much as it reveals.

The Sophists (those Peripatetics or travelling teachers) of Socrates' time knew this and taught rhetoric; they earned a living by making falsehoods seem plausible and convincing in their erroneous but effective logic. With them the practise of philosophy became playful; it lost its seriousness and commitment to ultimate truth. The lie became nuanced and textured.

The Sophists taught that truth was a nuisance and showed young men, through the powers of persuasion, how a weak argument could defeat a strong argument, how falsehood could win out against fact by employing various rhetorical tricks and devises much as one would do when debating or defending in court. In his dialogue *Euthydemus*, Plato shows up the subtleties of such strategies. In it, two mischievous professors attempt to demonstrate to an impressionable and good-looking young man how some spurious so-called proofs can be presented as seemingly true through a series of verbal contortions. Plato wants to show up their specious fictions and to set out a sound logic that will safeguard truth. There were many men like Euthydemus and Dionysodorus in the Athenian Assembly who were famous for truth-twisting. Socrates, posing as a slow-witted simpleton who was baffled by such clever rhetorical devices, showed up such verbal word-play for what it was – sophistry and illusion. Protagoras, the Greek philosopher and mathematician, had gone so far as to say that it is not possible to think what is false since a person can only think what he experiences and this can never be false. With the Sophists, fantasy and fiction became fused. Xenophon, another Greek philosopher and admirer of Socrates, called them prostitutes; they were paid chasers after the young and wealthy, as Plato called them in *The Sophist*. Rhetoric replaced Wisdom. Little has changed since those far-off Greek days. Gossip has not gone away. We still prefer rumour to reality. Aristotelian logic is still taught in philosophy departments; rhetoric is still practised in courtrooms and in university debating chambers, and people still lie, cheerfully and convincingly, poorly or proficiently.

• •

'Truly, to tell lies is not honorable;
but when the truth entails tremendous ruin,
to speak dishonorably is pardonable.'
– Sophocles (496 BC–406 BC)

• •

The Lies We Tell

There are countless different lies: we lie through our teeth, to use one expression (lying really well, or perhaps just forcibly); misleading; dissembling (here one presents the facts in a way that is literally true but intentionally misleading); big lies; bad faith; barefaced or bald-faced lies; brazen lies; white lies; scarlet lies; noble lies; bluffing; bullshitting; Butler lies (small lies usually sent electronically, which are used to terminate conversations or to save face); poker faces; contextual lies; being economical with the truth; strategic or emergency lies; irony; teasing; exaggerating; embellishing; sarcasm; tall tales; jocose lies (meant just in jest); stretching the truth; fabrication (for example, giving directions to a tourist when the person doesn't actually know the directions); fibbing; false compliments and reassurances ('That looks very nice on you' or 'Everything's going to be alright'); perjury; puffery; a pack of lies, porky pies, and so on.

These are the lies we tell; we tell them to others and sometimes we even lie to ourselves either knowingly ('no, our relationship will be fine; there's no cause to worry' as we blithely go about our business ignoring the problems lurking there) or unconsciously, in that, in this case, the lie has become so powerful and prevalent that we are convinced that it's the truth. Here, the illusion comes near to being a delusion. I guess what separates the 'normal' neurotic (most of us) from the psychotic (madman) is one of degrees in that the former usually know when they're lying whereas the latter lives the lie so it becomes their truth. For example, when we say 'I'm God' we are usually joking (hopefully); when the psychotic says it he believes it; he is suffering from delusions; we, by contrast, are engaging in wish-fulfilments. Either way, we are not going to be hauled off in a straight-jacket. This raises the interesting question about the relationship between lies and mental illness. The question is: Can a psychotic person lie?

• •

**'In this treacherous world
Nothing is the truth nor a lie.
Everything depends on the color
Of the crystal through which one sees it.'
– Pedro Calderón de la Barca**

• •

The Lies of Madmen

We can't cure a madman with our truth; they won't believe us – there is just no convincing them – probably just as well. To take an example that Slavok Žižek, the contemporary Slovenian philosopher, cites: a man who believes himself to be a grain of seed (the lie: he's not, he's a man but clearly he doesn't know he's lying) is taken to a mental hospital where the doctor does his best to tell him the truth – that he is not a seed but a man. When he is 'cured' and convinced that he is a man and allowed to leave the institution, he immediately comes back inside shaking. There is a chicken outside the door and he's afraid it will eat him. The doctor says, 'My good man, you know very well that you're a man and not a grain of seed'. The man replies, 'Of course I know that, but does the chicken know it?'

The unconscious itself (in this case, the psychotic's unconscious) must be brought to assume the truth; it is not enough to convince others about their unconscious truth. The question is: how to do it? How do you go about convincing others that their visual or auditory hallucinations are precisely that: hallucinations? So the psychotic lies from our perspective but from his perspective he is telling the truth. Sometimes a literal tell-

14

ing of truth is a sign or symptom of psychopathology, of mental abnormality. Autistic children are unable to lie; they cannot pretend or conceal. Similarly, the psychotic has repressed nothing and so has no secrets he keeps from himself. Those with Parkinson's disease show difficulties too in deceiving others. There is a term for compulsive lying: *pseudologia fantastica*. *Mythomania* is the term used to designate and describe an excessive propensity for lying. And did you know that speech is shorter when lying than when telling the truth? Lies tend to be tight, just as truth is tangential.

The above discussion touches on an interesting topic raised by Friedrich Nietzsche, the German philosopher, whom we quoted in the Preface, and it is this: is all truth fiction? Is all fiction interpretation? Is truth merely a perspective? (We considered above the case of the psychotic whose 'truth' is our lie; does this mean that our lies are his truths?) If I don't see twelve pink elephants running around the room and he does I would say I am sane and he is insane but we have to distinguish between material (physical) and mental (psychical) reality, so what 'reality' are we talking about? Perhaps we see the same world but see it differently to each other? Partial truths and truthful lies, so. Let's go into the matter in a little bit more detail.

Lies with Truth

Every truth is partial; truth is a perspective (this according to Nietzsche). If this is true then is every lie a partial truth? 'Why are you saying you're glad to see me, when you're really glad to see me?' One can be too suspicious. Sometimes we do mean what we say. Imagine. 'Say what you mean.' If only! Protect me from what I want. I just might get it. If someone says (consciously), 'Don't lie to me', they may very well mean (unconsciously), 'Please lie to me'. It's like the proverbial patient who came to Freud, who questioned him about his dream, and said, 'I can tell you one thing for definite – it's not about my mother.' Guess what? It's about his mother!

In 1873 Nietzsche wrote, 'On Truth and Lies in a Non-Moral Sense', in which he offers a number of subtle reflections on the psychology of lying, ones that were to influence Freud and his creation of psychoanalysis. According to Nietzsche, the art of dissimulation reaches its peak in man:

• •

'Deception, flattering, lying, deluding,
talking behind the back, putting up a
false front, living in borrowed splendour,
wearing a mask, hiding behind convention,
playing a role for others and for oneself,
.... is so much the rule and law among
men that there is almost nothing which is
less comprehensible than how an honest
and pure drive for truth could have arisen
among them. They are deeply immersed
in illusions and in dream images; .... man
permits himself to be deceived in
his dreams every night of his life.'

• •

So even dreams deceive; they lie themselves. Freud held this too – that every dream is a disguise, a distortion, a deception intent on leading us astray. The unconscious itself can't lie, but a dream is not the same as the unconscious. For psychoanalysts, consciousness is deceptive. What then is truth? In a famous passage, Nietzsche describes truth as a 'movable host of metaphors, metonymies, ... Truths are illusions which we have forgotten are illusions – they are metaphors that have become worn out'. And in his book, *Human, All Too Human*, Nietzsche wonders whether convictions are even more dangerous enemies to truth than lies. There is one fundamental difference between the 'normal' neurotic (as I am calling most of us) and the psychotic in this regard: we doubt things whereas the psychotic is certain. He just knows. Convictions can be very stubborn and extremely hard to shift even in the face of incontrovertible truth to the contrary. In *The Antichrist*, Nietzsche puts the question more definitively and we are not left wondering as to his answer:

• •

'Is there any actual difference between a lie and a conviction?' What a lie is in the father can become a conviction in the son. Lying is thus akin to a conviction: 'I call it lying to refuse to see what one sees, or to refuse to see it as it is: .... The most common sort of lie is that by which a man deceives himself.'

• •

Nietzsche felt that lying is more natural than truth-telling. Goethe, the German playwright, had likewise opined that, 'Truth is contrary to our nature' in his *Maxims and Reflections*. In his 1873 thesis, Nietzsche had gone as far as to say that truth cannot even be recognised. For him, the pleasure of lying is artistic and artistic pleasure 'speaks the truth quite generally in the form of lies'. Interestingly, for Richard Rorty, the American philosopher, truth is opposed not to falsehood but to pleasure. Later, Oscar Wilde would scandalise Victorian society with his Nietzschean aphorisms and epigrams (and we shall read his reflections on the subject later on as well). For Nietzsche, truth can be a cloak to disguise different drives and desires. Truth can be selfish, sinister, a smoke screen for subversive and submerged intentions. Freud, a sometime follower of Nietzsche, wrote in a letter to Arnold Zweig (31 May 1936) that 'truth is unobtainable; humanity does not deserve it'.

The minute someone says, 'Truth is here', if it is proclaimed by Confucius or Mohammed or the Christian Church, 'the priest lies', as no one has 'the Truth'. All we have are truths – lower case and pluralised; Nietzsche calls it the 'holy lie' and to believe in God is the ultimate, the 'longest lie' (for both Nietzsche and Sartre). If, to believe in God is to lie to ourselves, for these atheists the question becomes for René Descartes, the French philosopher and believer: does God deceive us? Let's see what he has to say on the subject. Some might say that Descartes put 'the cart before the horse'. I know, dreadful joke.

Does God Deceive Us?

Descartes, for a while at least, entertained the thought that perhaps God could deceive him, that God could be an evil genius, a malignant rather than benevolent deity, a thesis he ultimately rejected. If God is all perfect (a common enough description or definition of God), He can't deceive us as deception implies imperfection.

We are told in numerous places in the Bible that God cannot lie (Num. 23: 19; Ps. 89: 35; Hab. 2: 3; Heb. 6: 13-18), but there are also examples of God lying (2 Thes. 2: 11; 1 Kings 22: 23; Ezek. 14: 9). The eighth commandment tells us not to bear false witness against our neighbour. There are, however, instances of lying in both the Old and New Testaments. Rahab lied to the King of Jericho; Delilah accused Samson of lying to her; Abraham tells his wife Sarah to lie to the Egyptians. And Jesus Christ refers to the Devil as the father of lies (John 8: 44). Satan, we are told, was a liar from the beginning. And St. Paul commands Christians: 'Do not lie to one another' (Colossians 3: 9). Now I just want to bring these quotations to your attention without delving into the intricacies of a theological debate on the subject. It seems logical enough (logical to me, at any rate) that if God exists He is good and therefore wouldn't lie or choose to deceive us. I, for one, would have no interest in a God who toys with or lies to us. 'As flies to wanton boys so are we to the gods; they kill us for their sport,' as *King Lear's* Gloucester says. Who would be interested in this type of lying, deceiving fiend? Either God is good or God is not, surely? Well, we now move from gods to dogs. We know that we humans lie and that God, if He exists, doesn't (don't we?). The question now is: Do animals lie?

The Lies of Animals

Nature is a liar. There is in nature and the animal kingdom a huge propensity for cheating. In the survival of the fittest (which means the destruction of the weakest), deceitfulness becomes an ethic. In this depressing Darwinian picture, creatures must camouflage (nature's craftiest trick) themselves from beastly, permissive predators who want to snack on them. There is mimicry and masquerade in butterflies, birds and beetles, in flora and fauna. Deliberate deceit, camouflage, concealment and cunning is more the rule than the exception as falsehood emerges through natural selection, variation and chance mutation. Play, pretence and poker faces are practised. As Heraclitus, the ancient Hellenic philosopher, once observed: 'Nature loves to hide.' Think of the changing colouration of some creatures for purposes of brute survival – 'nature red in tooth and claw'. Certain animals and insects change their colour or their coats. When threatened, the hognose snake likes to fake its own death by emitting foul odours and hanging its tongue out of its mouth, producing drops of blood as it does. The cheetah (cheater), though, never changes his spots. But do animals have the mental ability to lie?

The capacity to lie has been claimed to be possessed by non-human animals in language studies with great apes. Koko, the gorilla made famous for learning American sign-language, was once caught red-handed. After tearing a steel sink from the wall in the middle of a tantrum, she signed to handlers that the cat did it!

Deceptive body language such as feints that mislead as to the direction of attack or flight has been observed in many species including wolves. A mother bird deceives when she pretends to have a broken wing to divert the attention of a perceived predator – from the eggs in its nest to itself – notably the killdeer. In the human kingdom there are some little boys who cry 'wolf' too many times to be believed. And there are, as we know, human wolves in sheep's clothes. Such cheating animals are chameleons just as some men are lizards in love.

Most animals leave tracks in their wake. Hunters look at these tracks to discover where their prey will be. The animal doesn't efface his trace. A select few will make false tracks designed to fool the hunter. But some hunters will know that the tracks they see are signs that the animals did not pass this way. Humans, however, set real tracks that are intended to signal that they have not gone in the direction they suggest. We can tell the truth to lie.

There is untruth at the heart of truth (for example, insects who appear to be part and parcel of the foliage).

What, though, is the difference between man, understood as a 'rational animal' to give him Aristotle's famous definition, and a non-human animal? An animal can feign but man can feign to feign. In other words, men lie in the guise of truth itself (we will see in detail what this means later). Such a man is like the Jew from an anecdote quoted by Freud:

• •

'Two friends meet on a train and one says to the other that he is going to Warsaw, to which his friend replies: "Why are you telling me you're going to Warsaw so I'll think you're going to Lemberg, when you are really going to Warsaw?"'

• •

It acts as a double bluff. By telling the truth ('I'm sorry I am late home but I swear I wasn't playing golf; I'm actually having an affair with a co-worker') while pretending to lie you're really telling the truth. This would be in a world where everybody lied. Similarly, we could say, 'Why are you complimenting me when you really mean it?' Or, as Groucho Marx famously said: 'He may act like an idiot and look like an idiot, but don't let that fool you. He really is an idiot.'

The Politics of Lying

Lying is universal. Should we always doubt what is being said to us? No, but we probably should take a lot of what we hear with a pinch of salt seeing how ubiquitous 'the lie' is. Telling the truth, after all, put Socrates, Jesus Christ and St. Thomas More, to cite but three examples, to death. In George Orwell's *1984*, a person who dared to speak the truth was liquidated by the State. There is, so, a politics of lying and of truth-telling. Politics is, after all, the art of the possible. And, at times, it is very difficult to distinguish between them. Life is lies, half-truth and evasion. We live in an age when trust is hard currency. We are lied to every day by the media, advertisers, lovers, friends and politicians (surely not?). As one unknown source says: 'How can you tell if a politician is lying? When his lips are moving.' Margaret Thatcher ruled out deliberate lies (she says) but ruled in the necessity of being evasive (she would). Alexander Haig, former General and US Secretary of State, defended this thus: 'That's not a lie; it's a terminological inexactitude. Also, a tactical misrepresentation.' Wow! Spin doctors, politicians, estate agents and advertising executives spin webs of deceit and like flies to spiders' webs we become entangled in their lies (mainly because we want to believe them ourselves). There is sham, sly evasions, artifice, cunning, chicanery, duplicity, dissimulation, disambiguation, bluff, guile, trickery, imposture, subterfuge, mystification and manipulativeness everywhere. Eve's serpent continues to tempt. But lies can convey truth; a pinch of lies can make the truth more palatable.

Freud took what his patients said with a pinch of salt realising that lies are sometimes more informative than the literal truth. There can also be a blurred line between fact and fantasy or fiction. Imagine that there are two doors with two guards standing outside. One door leads to Hell, the other to Paradise. One guard always lies and the other always tells the truth. (In some versions of this story, one door leads to the castle and the other door leads to certain death.) You have to find out which door leads to eternal happiness by asking one of the guards one question only. What question do you ask? In the 1986 fantasy film, *Labyrinth*, Sarah, the protagonist, asks: 'Would the other guard tell me that this door leads to the castle?' Clever. Unfortunately, in life we must contend with lying and truth-telling in the same person; and sometimes these two are uttered simultaneously. Sometimes, too, somebody is suffering from False Memory Syndrome. Here is the answer. Ask one guard: 'If I were to ask the other guard which door I should take to go to Paradise, which one would he tell me?' One then takes the other door from the one indicated.

The Lies of Children

So the question is: when does lying in the human animal first begin? Children used to chant 'liar, liar, pants on fire'. Remember that one? Children lie from three years of age onwards and lying develops rapidly after that. At four and a half years they begin to lie convincingly. By age seven, children are pretty proficient at lying, showing a Machiavellian intelligence. Now, where do they get that from, Mummy or Daddy? But the question is: left to their own devices would children lie at all or, rather, are their lies responses to the lies of adults? Frequently they are. All adults lie to children and all children want is the truth. Lucky for them they don't get it. Goethe wryly observed, 'Children are a real touchstone of what is falsehood and what is truth. They have far less need for self-deception than do old people.' Indeed.

In 'Two Lies Told by Children' (1913), Freud opines that children tell lies when they are imitating the lies told by adults. But children can tell lies under the influence of excessive feelings of love, and Freud gives two such examples. I warn you, they are a bit intricate – psychoanalysis always is.

The first case concerns a girl of seven, in her second year at school, who asked her father for some money in order to buy colours to paint some Easter eggs. Her father refused, saying he had no money to spare. Later, she asked him for money for a wreath for the funeral of their reigning princess who had just died and to which each of the schoolchildren were contributing sixpence. Her father gave her ten marks (ten shillings, in the old money, we are helpfully told): she paid her contribution, put nine marks on her father's writing-table and with the remaining money bought paints which she hid in her toy cupboard. At dinner her father asked her what she did with the missing money and whether she had, in fact, bought paints with it. She lied; she denied it altogether but her older brother, who was nine years old, betrayed her and the paints were found. The angry father gave her over to her mother who punished her severely, we are told.

After this, the girl fell into despair, which shook up her mother. The mother tried everything to console the girl but this once self-confident and wild child had become shy and timid. She herself described this event in her life as a 'turning-point'. Years later, when she was engaged to be married and her mother purchased her furniture for her she flew into a rage, which at the time she didn't understand. She had feelings that it was her money and no one else ought to buy anything with it. As a wife she was reluctant to ask her husband for any money for herself and made an unnecessary distinction between his money and hers.

During the course of her psychoanalysis, her husband's money was delayed in reaching her and as a consequence she was left without resources in a foreign city. Freud made her promise him that if this happened again she would borrow from him (can't see any analyst I know doing this). She promised to do so but when she was again in a state of 'financial embarrassment' she pawned her jewellery instead. She said she couldn't take money from Freud. Her analysis progressed and revealed some interesting facts.

Sometime before she went to school she played a similar prank with money. A neighbour had sent the girl out with some money in the company of her own boy, who was younger, to buy something in the shops. She was bringing the change back home but when she met the neighbour's servant in the street she flung the money on the pavement. When, in analysis, she recalled this, the thought of Judas occurred to her, who threw down thirty pieces of silver, which he had been given for betraying Christ. But how did she identify with Judas?

When she was a little over three years of age she had a nursemaid of whom she was exceedingly fond. This girl had become involved in an affair with a doctor whose surgery she visited with the child. The child had witnessed various sexual proceedings. It wasn't certain if she saw the doctor give the girl – the nursemaid – money but it was certain that the girl gave the child some money in order to buy her silence. It is possible that the doctor also gave the child money. However, the child betrayed the nursemaid to her mother out of jealousy, we are told. She played with the coins in such an obvious and ostentatious manner that the mother became curious and enquired about the coins and the nursemaid was dismissed.

So, to take money from anybody meant, for her, an erotic relation and to take money from her father was equivalent to a declaration of love, Freud contended. The phantasy that her father was her lover was so seductive that her wish for paints for her Easter eggs put itself into effect despite the parental prohibition. She disavowed the fact that she had appropriated the money because her motive (unconscious) for the deed could not be admitted. Her father's punishment was a rejection of her love, a humiliation that 'broke her spirit'. Freud tells us that during the treatment a period of severe depression occurred when on one occasion Freud was obliged to reproduce the humiliation by requesting that she not bring him any more flowers.

The second case involved a woman who was very ill because of a 'frustration' in life. We are told that she was truth-loving, serious and virtuous in her earlier years and became an affectionate wife (interestingly, Freud had inserted 'and happy' at this point but then had taken it out).

Earlier still, in the first years of her life, she had been a wilful and discontented child and though she had changed into a good girl, there were occurrences in her schooldays that caused her guilt. Her memory told her that in those days she had often boasted and lied. Once she told a classmate that they had 'ice' at dinner, ice, in fact, every day. In reality she didn't know what ice at dinner meant. She only knew ice from the long blocks in which it was carted but assumed there was something 'grand' in having it for dinner.

When she was ten years old she had to do a free drawing of a circle in one of her drawing lessons but she used a pair of compasses instead and produced a perfect circle and boasted to everyone about it. This incurred the questioning of the girl by the teacher but she 'stubbornly' denied what she had done and took refuge in 'sullen silence'. No further steps were taken in the matter.

Both the above lies were instigated by the same complex. As the eldest of five children the girl had developed a strong attachment to her father 'which was destined when she was grown up to wreck her happiness in life'. She couldn't escape the discovery though that her beloved father was not such a great person as he was inclined to think. He had to struggle with money difficulties and he wasn't so powerful or distinguished as he imagined. But she could not tolerate this departure from her ideal. 'Since as women do, she based all her ambition on the man she loved, she became too strongly dominated by the motive of supporting her father against the world. So she boasted to her schoolfellows, in order not to have to belittle her father. When, later on, she learned to translate ice for dinner by "glace", her self-reproaches about this reminiscence led her by an easy path into a pathological dread of pieces or splinters of glass.' (The German *glas*, like 'glass' in English, has a similar sound to the French for 'ice' – *glace*).

Her father was an excellent draughtsman and had excited the admiration of the children with exhibitions of his skill. It was an identification of herself with her father that she had drawn the circle at school. It was as though she wanted to boast, 'look at what my father can do'. The sense of guilt that was attached to her excessive fondness for her father found its expression in connection with her attempted deception; an admission that was impossible for the same reason that was given in the first example – it would have been 'an admission of her hidden incestuous love'. Despite the psychoanalytical intricacies of these case histories, Freud showed the importance of the unconscious in the life of the human person and that the truth can come out in our lies, slips, symptoms, bungled actions, jokes and dreams at night. The unconscious betrays us daily. Yes, we lie all the time. But the truth can be rediscovered in these formations of the unconscious.

The neurotic (that's us by the way, well, most of us) represses the truth, which can be all too ugly, altogether too grotesque. In psychoanalysis, the patient promises to tell the truth, however, even as he lies on the couch

but the full truth can't be spoken. The unconscious bars such knowledge. We forget, fail to recall correctly, omit. Nobody can promise to speak the truth, the whole truth and nothing but the truth. Let us hope, therefore, that we are not taken to court. Of course, law is not justice.

Even when we are lying we are operating in the domain and dimension of the truth. Truth and lying are two sides of the same coin, of a 'Moebius strip'. In an early work by Freud, entitled *The Psychopathology of Everyday Life* (1901), Freud said this:

• •

'It may, in general, seem astonishing that the urge to tell the truth is so much stronger than is usually supposed. Perhaps, however, my being scarcely able to tell lies any more is a consequence of my occupation with psychoanalysis.'

• •

Perhaps the consistency of lies changes during the course (curse?) of an analysis? Maybe they become lighter to bear. Perhaps the lie (as if there were just the one) permits the patient to avoid or evade suffering pain? There are different faces of lies: little lies and large lies, to begin with. We need to distinguish between them.

Big Lies and Little Lies

L et us designate little lies as 'lies' and large lies as 'Lies'. The former are understandable, permissible and I would say creative – there is great originality in lying after all. Big lies are problematic and can be dangerous; the lie can become the truth in society. We saw in the last century how this led to Nazism and the horrors of the Holocaust. We were told that Jews were not people; on the contrary, they were vermin who had to be exterminated. This was the ultimate lie spoken in those dark and dreadful days. The Russian writer, Alexander Solzhenitsyn, who experienced the inside of a Gulag, understandably exhorted 'live not by lies!' But this was the big Lie that became a society's truth. It was pernicious propaganda that spread throughout the derailed and distorted society that was Hitler's Germany. But it was a lie believed by a large portion of the people – for a while, at least (they wanted to hear the lie). Truth, though, won out in the end because whatever about lying to others we can't continue to lie to ourselves; at some point we must face the fact that the lie we created, that is, the Jew as less than human, is an act of collective scapegoating and psychological projection.

Isn't a falsity the lack of truth, of authentication, the lack of harmony between words, ideas and things? In logic, truth is the correct fit between a thought and a reality; falsity is its unsuitability. To lie is to induce a falsity, to make something look like something else. (Jews portrayed or depicted as less than human). Jeering Pilate asked Jesus Christ, 'what is Truth?', but didn't wait but for an answer. Some people just don't want to hear the truth. (And there Truth was, standing before Pontius Pilate Himself: 'I am the Way, the Truth and the Life'.) Truth, in logic, is the correspondence of a statement and that to which the statement refers, to the reality it names. Isn't the Truth unknowable? If it is, any formulation of this truth made by a human being would thus be a falsity. A falsity would, therefore, be the only possibility the human mind has of stating and communicating the truth. The lie transforms the truth. In order to lie, one first must have been in touch with the truth. The lie would seem to be a normal part of our mental functioning. Perhaps lying is a way of preventing us from becoming mad. And who hasn't lied? Babies who haven't yet learnt language. Speaking of silence, of lying silence, imagine this. Your friend or lover goes to hug you and you say: 'I really love you,' and they say ... nothing. Isn't this the 'sin of omission'? 'According to Robert Louis Stevenson, the Scottish novelist:

• •

'The cruelest lies are often told in silence.
A man may have sat in a room for hours
and not opened his mouth, and yet come
out of that room a disloyal friend or
a vile calumniator.'

• • • • • • • • • • • • • • •

Below is an example from Woody Allen of all the things we keep concealed but think about, even as we speak.

Lying With Woody Allen

In his film *Annie Hall*, Woody Allen has a conversation with Ms. Hall. As they are talking to each other, each of them is thinking something that they are not saying (lies of silence/sins of omission). They may not be literally lying but they are not telling the truth. The conversation goes like this:

Allen: 'So did you do those photographs in there or what?'

Hall: 'I sort of dabble round'. (She thinks: 'I dabble? Listen to me – what a jerk'.)

Allen: 'They're wonderful; they have a quality'. (He thinks: 'You're a great-looking girl.')

Hall: 'I would like to take a serious photography course'. (She thinks: 'He probably thinks I'm a yo-yo.')

Allen: 'Photography's interesting – it's a new art form, and a set of aesthetic criteria has not emerged yet'. (He thinks: 'I wonder what she looks like naked?')

Hall: 'Aesthetic criteria? You mean whether it's a good fake or not?' (She thinks: 'I'm not smart enough for him. Hang in there.')

Allen: 'The medium enters in as a condition of the art form itself.' (He thinks: 'I don't know what I'm saying – she senses I'm shallow.')

Hall: 'Well, to me, I mean, it's all instinctive. I mean I just try to feel it, try to get a sense of it, not think about it so much.' (She thinks: 'God, I hope he doesn't turn out to be a shmuck like the others.')

Allen: 'Still, you need a set of aesthetic guidelines to put it in social perspective.' (He thinks: 'Christ, I sound like FM radio. Relax.')

This is typical of friends and lovers (in the above, Allen and Hall lie out of anxiety) and is illustrative of at least two things: 1) the missed encounter between two people, who 2) don't say what they really mean. It is typical of communication, which operates by way of miscommunication. Don't we speak in order not to be understood? If we were so completely understood by each other there would be no need to speak. Ethical lying: to save some good. Golden silence: born of fear.

Later, Annie Hall asks Woody Allen does he love her. He says love is too weak a word and jokingly elongates the word: 'I loove you', etc. In other words, he doesn't answer. So quite obviously he doesn't reciprocate her feelings for him. But he doesn't say this. He realises the truth is hard to hear and handle so he fudges the issue and avoids the answer. He commits an act of 'bad faith', as Sartre would have it. Bad faith or good intentions? Don't all lovers lie? And commit acts of bad faith? Let's see what Sartre says on the subject. I warn you, dear reader, this section requires some concentration as it is a bit convoluted. It's not for the faint-hearted. So pour yourself a stiff drink and take a deep breath. Another one. Ok, let's continue. Or you may want to skip this Sartrean section. I won't mind. Seriously.

Self-Deception

According to Demosthenes, 'Nothing is easier than self-deceit'. Dostoyevsky says:

● ●

**'Lying to ourselves is more deeply
engrained than lying to others ...
The important thing is to stop
lying to ourselves.'**

● ● ● ● ● ● ● ● ● ● ● ● ● ● ● ● ●

Yes, but how? Frequently Sartre's idea of *mauvaise foi* or 'bad faith' – sometimes translated as 'self-deception', as I have said said – is identified with falsehood. We say that a person 'shows signs of bad faith or that he lies to himself', as Sartre says in the section on 'bad faith' in his magnum opus, *Being and Nothingness*. Bad faith is a lie one tells to oneself. There is a difference, though, between lying to oneself and lying in general. For Sartre, 'lying is a negative attitude'. He explains:

• •

'The essence of the lie implies in fact that
the liar actually is in complete possession
of the truth which he is hiding. A man does
not lie about what he is ignorant of; he does
not lie when he spreads an error of which
he himself is the dupe; he does not lie when
he is mistaken. The ideal description of
the liar would be a cynical consciousness,
affirming truth within himself, denying it in
his words, and denying that negation as
such.... The liar intends to deceive
and he does not seek to hide this
intention from himself.'

• • • • • • • • • • • • • • • • • • • •

This is the ideal lie but often the liar is the victim
of his lie – 'he half persuades himself of it'. The lie is
a normal phenomenon, an inevitable product of our
'being-with-others' (as existentialist philosophers are
wont to say) in the world. In other words, the lie presupposes the existence of the Other (person). The lie,
so, is stitched into the very fabric of social life. All lies
are societal, to some extent at least.

In bad faith the one to whom the lie is told and the one who lies are the same person. This means that I am aware, as deceiver, of the truth which is hidden from me in my capacity as the one deceived. I know the truth very well in order to conceal it so carefully. But there is a problematic present. I know I am committing bad faith. I am conscious of my being in bad faith. So I must be in good faith to the extent that I am conscious of my bad faith. Get it?

Sartre gives many examples of people who are in bad faith. A girl goes to the doctor and cries, not because there is anything wrong but so that nothing may be wrong, in order not to have to talk to him (see Sartre's *Sketch for a Theory of the Emotions*).

Many attempts are made to escape from (the embarrassment of) bad faith: one is psychoanalysis, the other is religion, according to Sartre (who believed neither in God nor in unconscious mental processes). In psychoanalysis one has recourse to 'the unconscious' to escape and avoid responsibility, according to Sartre. Psychoanalysis would have us believe that the human subject deceives himself about everything. For example, an act of stealing is seen no longer as a simple act of stealing but as evidence of an unconscious act of self-punishment, for example. In psychoanalysis, so, there is no bad faith; what we now have, according to Sartre, is the idea of a lie without a liar.

I can, therefore, understand or appreciate how I can be lied to without lying to myself. Psychoanalysis puts no person in possession of himself. My 'superego' (Sartre said he didn't have one) or conscience censors the truth about myself but the censor must know what it is repressing for repression to take place, Sartre maintains. The censor must choose and must, so, be aware. It (consciously) comprehends the drives that are to be repressed (unconsciously). One knows and knows that one knows, says Sartre. 'All knowing is consciousness of knowing.' So the censor is conscious of itself when it is 'doing' the (unconscious) repressing. It involves consciousness of being conscious of the drive to be repressed in order not to be conscious of it. This means, Sartre concludes, that the censor is in bad faith. Id, ego and superego become 'mere verbal terminologies'. Ultimately, bad faith is, for Sartre, what the unconscious and the censor are for Freud.

Next, Sartre enquires: 'What must be the being of man if he is to be capable of bad faith?' He gives an example by way of illustration. A man invites a woman out to dine. They are in the restaurant. She knows his intentions; she also knows that she is going to have to choose one way or the other. She doesn't know what she wants and treats his word and sentences, for example, 'I find you attractive', as mere words and mere sentences; she disarms them of their sexual connotations and background. She is aware of the desire she

inspires, excites, ignites. She wants, though, to be recognised and appreciated in her full freedom, that is
to say, in her complete subjectivity. Now suppose he
grasps her hand. This risks changing the situation since
something has happened and it requires, necessitates,
an immediate decision on her behalf. To leave the hand
there is to consent to flirt; to withdraw it is to break the
charm and harmony of the hour. Her aim: to postpone
the moment of deciding for as long as is possible. What
happens next? She leaves her hand there but isn't aware
she is leaving it there. At that moment 'she is all intel-
lect'. Sartre unravels it thus: 'She draws her companion
up to the most lofty regions of sentimental speculation;
she speaks of life, of her life; she shows herself in her
essential aspect – a personality, a consciousness. And
during this time the divorce of the body from the soul is
accomplished; the hand rests inert between the warm
hands of her companion – neither consenting nor re-
sisting – a thing' – a thing resting. This woman is in
bad faith. She uses various devices to maintain this bad
faith.

So, is sincerity the opposite of bad faith? Sincerity
seems to be the antithesis of bad faith. In sincerity, a
man is for himself only what he is. If man is what he
is, bad faith becomes impossible and 'candour ceases to
be his ideal and becomes instead his being'. But is man
what he is? Well, for Sartre, we must make ourselves
what we are. But then what are we if we have to keep

making ourselves what we are? He gives an example of a waiter in a café.

The waiter is in his café and his movements are quick but they are a little too rapid; he walks to his customers a little too quickly, bends forward a little too eagerly and his eyes express interest a little too solicitously. He walks imitating in his upright stiffness an automaton as he carries his tray with the recklessness of a tight-rope walker. His behaviour is like a game. He is playing but playing (at) what? He is playing at being a waiter in a café, according to Sartre. It is a ceremony, a ritual, a lie. And this is what the public demands. There is the dance of the grocer, the tailor, the auctioneer, 'by which they endeavour to persuade their clientele that they are nothing but a grocer, an auctioneer, a tailor. A grocer who dreams is offensive to the buyer, because such a grocer is not wholly a grocer. Society demands that he limit himself to his function as a grocer.' There are many precautions we take to imprison a person in what he is. We live in perpetual fear he just might escape from it, break away and elude his condition, Sartre contends. But the waiter in the café cannot be a café waiter in the sense that an inkwell is an inkwell or a glass is a glass. Sincerity, so, is really a task that is impossible to achieve. The waiter is always more than a waiter. The very meaning of sincerity is a contradiction. To be sincere is to be what one is and that presupposes I am not (originally) what I am. I can become sincere but not being what one is renders being what one is impossible. The attentive student is attempting to be attentive. Sincerity is, thus, impossible. How can we even attempt to be sincere in conversation or confession? The effort is 'doomed to failure'. I try to be what I am, decide or resolve to be my 'true self'; this means setting about and searching for ways to change myself, to not be me. If I am now the person I am, then in the past I wasn't. And that won't do at all. We are upset, says Sartre, when the penalties of the court 'affect a man who in his new freedom is no longer the guilty person he was. But at the same time we require of the man that he recognize himself as being this guilty one'. Sartre concludes: sincerity itself is a phenomenon of bad faith. Another example is given.

A homosexual has intolerable guilt and his whole existence is determined in relation to it. He is in bad faith. He has a certain conception of the beautiful that women will not satisfy. His friend, who is his critic too, is irritated with his 'duplicity', with is inability and refusal to consider himself 'a homosexual' even though he recognises his inclination and engages in homosexual acts. The critic wants him to declare himself. Who, Sartre asks, is in bad faith? 'The homosexual or the champion of sincerity?'

The homosexual recognises himself but doesn't want to be considered as a thing. He has the impression that a homosexual is not a homosexual as the table is a table or as the red-haired man is red-haired. He must

put himself beyond, must escape to live, to avoid judge-
ment. Yes, he is not what he is. Human reality can't be
completely or finally defined by patterns of conduct.
Fine, but he lays claim to not being homosexual in the
sense in which the table is not an inkwell and to that
extent he is in bad faith. The champion of sincerity
requires that he acknowledge himself in the name of
freedom and sincerity, as a homosexual. Such a 'confession' will win indulgence, he says to him. This means,
though, that the man who will acknowledge himself as a
homosexual will no longer be the same as the homosexual whom he acknowledges being. The critic demands
of him to be what he is in no longer being what he is.
The critic demands that he constitute himself as a thing
in order no longer to treat him as a thing. This 'contradiction is constitutive of the demand of sincerity'. We
now see how offensive to the Other and how reassuring
for me is the statement – 'he is just a homosexual'; this
constitutes all the acts of the Other as consequences following on from his essence. The critic (a false friend)
'is demanding of his victim – that he constitute himself as a thing, that he should entrust his freedom to
his friend as a fief'. The champion of sincerity is in bad
faith. The constant effort to adhere to oneself and be
sincere is actually to dissociate oneself from oneself. It
is to escape from oneself and the person who seeks to
escape from himself commits bad faith. So the goal of
sincerity and of bad faith isn't so different. I try to be

sincere and don't succeed, therefore. Sincerity always misses its mark. In order not to be cowardly I must be a little cowardly. It means being and not being a coward. Bad faith involves denying qualities that I possess but that's not all. It is not seeing the being I am but it also involves me in attempting to constitute myself as being what I am not. 'Thus in order for bad faith to be possible, sincerity itself must be in bad faith.' We are what we are not and not what we are. That is the paradox at the heart of contradictory and confused humanity.

Sartre says that his friend Pierre feels friendship for him and he believes this in good faith. He believes and trusts (in) it. He conducts himself as if he were certain of it. Such a faith is simple. To believe is to know one believes but to know one believes is no longer to believe. Believing is destructive of belief. 'To believe is not-to-believe.' Belief becomes non-belief. Just as the absolute becomes relative and the relative absolute. 'Every belief is a belief that falls short; one never wholly believes what one believes .... If every belief in good faith is an impossible belief, then there is a place for every impossible belief.' I believe I believe.

Bad faith is the basis of all and every faith. 'At the moment when I wish to believe myself courageous I know that I am a coward.' It is the acceptance of not believing what it believes that it is bad faith. Good faith flees this 'not-believing-what-one-believes'. 'In bad faith there is no cynical lie nor knowing preparation for deceitful concepts. But the very first act of bad faith is to flee what it can not flee, to flee what it is.' Bad faith denies itself as bad faith. Bad faith is a threat – permanent and possible – to every project of the human being. And the origin of this risk, according to Sartre, is the fact that it is the nature of consciousness to be what it is not and not to be what it is – a case, then, of being and nothingness. Authenticity would be self-recovery.

Just as I try to flee and free myself from the Other, he is trying to flee and free himself from me. While I seek to enslave him, the Other seeks to enslave me. There is no escape from this Other, from any and every Other. We live with Others in the world and this produces conflict, a Master-Slave struggle to the death. 'Conflict,' Sartre says, 'is the original meaning of being-for-others.' Therefore, 'love is a conflict' too. Conflict everywhere, so, in love and lies, of a love that lies. Speaking of love and lying lovers, let's consider this subject next, as we take leave of Sartre ('phew', I hear you say). Adieu Jean-Paul.

Love, Lies and Letters

The lies written in love letters: 'I will never leave you'; 'I will kill myself if you leave me'. If a woman writes a love letter she is usually addressing herself; that's 'why women write more letters than they post', to coin a phrase. If the first of April is a day when we officially sanction the lie, Valentine's Day is when we unofficially lie – it's a day for liars as much as lovers (the two tend to go hand in hand). It provides us with the greatest opportunity to lie in the calendar; it formalises and ritualises the art of lying. 'I love you. I can't exist without you', but in love, deeds speak louder than words. Who, dear reader, is your secret Valentine? 'Please don't lie to me, unless you're absolutely sure I'll never find out the truth' (Ashleigh Brilliant, English author) or 'Tell all the Truth but tell it slant' (Emily Dickinson, American poet).

We wear masks all the time, especially in love. A mask is not a total lie. But the mask may slip over too much wine: *in vino veritas*. Conscience is, after all, soluble in alcohol.

• •

**'Man is least himself when he talks in his
own person. Give him a mask and he
will tell you the truth.' – Oscar Wilde**

• •

But behind the mask (the *persona*, hence our word 'personality') lies the character.

Doesn't love only really work when we desire a second person to the one we love? Isn't it that desire that keeps our love alive? Can one really be in love with and desire the same person? It is desire that keeps a relationship alive not (just) love. And of course we can distinguish between sex (bodily/physical), eroticism (mental/psychological) and love (spiritual), though they can become muddied and muddled, as we know only too well. As for married life, well, didn't Oscar Wilde, the Irish wit, tell us that in married life three is company, two is none?! Lies keep marriages alive.

• •

**'Telling lies is a fault in a boy, an art in a
lover, an accomplishment in a bachelor, and
second nature in a married man.'
– Helen Rowland**

• • • • • • • • • • • • • •

• •

'The charm of marriage is that it makes a life of deception absolutely necessary for both parties.' – Oscar Wilde

• •

• •

'One can always recognise women who trust their husbands. They look so thoroughly unhappy.' – Oscar Wilde

• •

The secret wedding vow: 'for better or forget it!' A tale is told about three truthful husbands. Žižek gives this example of the simultaneous telling and sharing of truth and lies in the marital home:

Three friends are having a drink at a bar; the first one says, 'A terrible thing happened to me. At a travel agency I wanted to say "A ticket to Pittsburgh" and I said, "A picket to Tittsburgh!" The second man replied, 'That's nothing. At breakfast I wanted to say to my wife, "Could you pass the sugar please, honey" and what I said was, "You stupid fucking bitch, you've ruined my life!"' The third one concludes: 'Wait till you hear what happened to me. After gathering up my courage all night, I decided to say to my wife exactly what you said to yours, and I ended up saying, "Could you pass the sugar, honey?"'

Lying Eyes

The eyes can lie. Such desire in those lying eyes. Those who continue to believe with their eyes are the most in error. A paedophile who happens to be a priest and who preaches virtue is a hypocrite, but his words may prompt his parishioners to do good deeds. We must believe with our ears not with our eyes. Those who have ears to hear, let them hear! Shakespeare got it right again: 'Love looks not with the eyes but with the mind and therefore is wing'd Cupid painted blind.' Love is mental. Love shoots arrows, as well as blanks.

The other person's eyes act as mirrors; they mirror us back to ourselves. 'Mirror, mirror on the wall, who's the fairest of them all?' All mirrors (and mirroring eyes) lie; they play tricks on us. They distort the truth just as much as caricature paintings do. They reveal to us our distorted double. We never see ourselves as others see us. We have only seen mirror images of ourselves (that's not you in the mirror – it's an image of you which may or may not be a spitting image). But in love-relationships when women lie they have more to lose than men. Women are at risk of losing their partner whereas men are at risk of losing only themselves.

Wilde Lies

Speaking of mirrors, it is said that artists hold up a mirror to reality; yes, and they receive back its distorted truth. We know art is a lie (artful lies?); we pay to be lied to (just as others pray to be lied to) when we go to the cinema or theatre or when we read books of fiction. All men are liars, the Scottish philosopher David Hume opined, but poets are liars by profession; that is why Plato expelled them from his ideal state (*polis*). 'We have art in order not to die of the truth' (Nietzsche).

According to Pablo Picasso:

● ●

'We all know that Art is not truth. Art is a lie that makes us realize truth at least the truth that is given us to understand. The artist must know the manner whereby to convince others of the truthfulness of his lies.'

● ● ● ● ● ● ● ● ● ● ● ● ● ● ● ● ● ● ●

Indeed, art is possible only as a lie. And some people make an art-form out of lying. Oscar Wilde was one such man.

Wilde wanted to reveal art and conceal himself as artist but the truth came out in the end and he suffered for it. He promised to tell the truth at his trial when he swore on a Bible and then lied about the exact nature of his involvement with all those boys, and he did it beautifully in that fine and famous speech from the dock; he forged a fabulous tissue of lies. He realised this from prison: 'A man whose desire is to be something separate from himself, to be a Member of Parliament, or a successful grocer, or a prominent solicitor, or a judge, or something equally tedious, invariably succeeds in being what he wants to be. That is his punishment. Those who want a mask have to wear it.'

He was shallow; becoming deeper is the privilege of suffering. But when one is alone, with no audience, one has to 'take the mask off for breathing purposes'. The mask makes lying easy. 'Truth ... is a thing which is most painful to listen to and most painful to utter'. A man's highest moment is when he kneels in the dust and meets, not the mask, but himself face to face and this too is what happened to Mr. Oscar Fingal O' Flahertie Wills Wilde. It is true that great passions are for the great of soul but every pleasure is paid for in the end. Wilde's life was broken in pieces by a lie but in prison he had to sit quietly in the silence of his cell and consider it to the full – his life, his loves, the death of his beloved mother whose funeral he was not permitted to attend, Lord Alfred Douglas' betrayal, his bankruptcy, divorce and the loss of his two lovely boys but 'to love all things are easy' and there 'is no prison in any world into which love cannot force an entrance'.

Bosie (as Lord Alfred was nicknamed), a British lord, came to this Irish playwright to learn about pleasure. In the concluding sentence to *De Profundis*, Wilde says to him that perhaps he is chosen to teach him now another lesson, something much more wonderful – 'the meaning of sorrow and its beauty' – the play of pain.

I was saying that Wilde played a terrible game with masks and attempted to conceal the truth about himself. To lie was easier. In fact, he wrote an essay entitled 'The Truth of Masks: A Note on Illusion' but that was before truth and prison caught up with him. The essay is an apologia of masks and lies. It is really an article on Shakespeare's plays, just as Wilde's 'The Portrait of Mr. W.H.' is an article on Shakespeare's sonnets. Shakespeare toyed with masks too, for dramatic effect. Wilde tells us: 'Posthumus hides his passion under a peasant's garb, and Edgar his pride beneath an idiot's rags; Portia wears the apparel of a lawyer.... Jessica felles from her father's house in boy's dress; .... Henry the Eighth woos his lady as a shepherd.'

Macbeth appears in a nightgown as if aroused from sleep. Dress here is used as dissimulation, disguise, deceit. Apparel and adornment are used for the purposes of camouflage and concealment. In Shakespeare's *Othello*, Iago drops hints the whole time and messes with Othello's jealous mind. A well-placed handkerchief leads to strangulation. There are Iagos all around us and more trickery than truth in the universe of man.

In this essay Wilde asserts: 'Truth is independent of facts always' and concludes thus:

• •

'For in art there is no such thing as a universal truth. A Truth in art is that whose contradictory is also true. And just as it is only in art-criticism, and through it, that we can apprehend the Platonic theory of ideas, so it is only in art-criticism, and through it, that we can realise Hegel's system of contraries. The truths of metaphysics are the truths of masks.'

• •

But it was in his 'The Decay of Lying: An Observation' that he sets out, in dialogue form, a conversation on the subject between Cyril and Vivian (the names of Wilde's two sons). The scene is the library of a country-house in Nottinghamshire.

Cyril admonishes Vivian for cooping himself up all day in the library and says: 'Let us go and lie on the grass and smoke cigarettes and enjoy Nature.' So the essay begins with a pun: Cyril wants to lie on the grass but Vivian feels that Nature is too uncomfortable, too hard, lumpy and damp and opines that Nature hates thought just as England does, where 'thought is not catching'. Vivian is writing an article and presently correcting the proofs. He is intending to call it, 'The Decay of Lying: A Protest', to which Cyril exclaims: 'Lying! I should have thought that our politicians kept up that habit.' Vivian disagrees, making the point that politicians never rise above mere misrepresentation:

•••••••••••••••••••••••••••••••••••

'How different from the temper of the true liar, with his frank, fearless statements, his superb irresponsibility, his healthy, natural disdain of proof of any kind! After all, what is a fine lie? Simply that which is its own evidence. If a man is sufficiently unimaginative to produce evidence in support of a lie, he might just as well speak the truth at once'.

•••••••••••••••••••••••

If the politicians don't really lie, barristers do better. Members of the Bar are prone to being sophistic (the subject on which we began this book). The mantle of the sophist, as Vivian (Wilde himself) says, has fallen on its members. 'Their feigned ardours and unreal rhetoric are delightful.' But the 'truth will out'. Even newspapers can now be relied upon. So there is not much going, in terms for lying, in relation to the lawyer or the journalist. Besides, what Vivian is pleading for is lying in art and it is intended for 'The Tired Hedonists', a club to which he belongs. He proceeds to read his article to the attentive Cyril. It begins by bemoaning the decay of lying as an art, science and social pleasure. Whereas the ancient historians gave us fiction in the form of fact, the modern novelist presents us with dull facts under the guise of fiction and hasn't the courage even of other people's ideas. Vivian holds that there is no such person as a 'born liar' or a 'born poet'. Both poetry and lying are arts that can be learned (Wittgenstein makes this point too); moreover, they are arts 'as Plato saw, not unconcerned with each other – and they require the most careful study, the most disinterested devotion'. Painting and sculpture possess their subtle and secret forms of craft and colour. The poet is known by his fine music just as the liar is recognised by 'his rich rhythmic utterance'. He bemoans the fact that the fashion of lying has almost entirely fallen into disrepute. Exaggeration is surely preferable to accuracy in conversation? Being in the company of the aged and the well informed is fatal to man's imagination, and in a short time he develops 'a morbid and unhealthy faculty of truth-telling'. It is the modern vice. Indeed, moralists have dreary vices and drearier virtues. Realism is a failure. Wilde prefers those persons who have the wit to exaggerate and the genius to romance. Speaking through his character Vivian, he says that he is 'tired of the intelligent person whose reminiscences are always based upon memory, whose statements are invariably limited by probability, and who is at any time liable to be corroborated by the merest Philistine who happens to be present. Society sooner or later must return to its lost leader, the cultured and fascinating liar'.

It is the liar, with his tall tales, who is the real founder of social intercourse.

Art is the breaking free from the 'prison-house' (Wilde ironically calls it) of realism. Art, indeed, will go forth to greet the liar, 'and will kiss his false, beautiful lips, knowing that he alone is in possession of the great secret of her manifestations, the secret that Truth is entirely and absolutely a matter of style; while Life – poor, probable, uninteresting human life' will meekly follow after him while miserably attempting to reproduce the marvels of which he speaks. Vivian goes on to say that undoubtedly there will be the critic who will contact the *Saturday Review* and censure the teller of fairy-tales (Wilde himself wrote some beautiful ones) and chide him for his defective knowledge of history; in their unimaginative way, they 'will hold up their ink-stained hands in horror'. In fact, they may even cite Shakespeare's aphorism that art holds the mirror up to nature but this particular epigram was put into the mouth of Hamlet to convince the bystanders of the insanity in matters of art. Art is a veil rather than a mirror, Vivian asserts, while Cyril asks for another cigarette. Far from art imitating life, life imitates art. Life is the mirror and art the reality. And Wilde was true to his philosophy. He made of his life a work of art:

● ●

'For the aim of the liar is simply to charm, to delight, to give pleasure. He is the very basis of civilised society, and without him a dinner-party, even at the mansions of the great, is as dull as a lecture at the Royal Society, or a debate at the Incorporated Authors.'

● ● ● ● ● ● ● ● ● ● ● ● ● ● ● ● ● ● ● ●

Vivian/Wilde makes the interesting point that to look at something is very different from seeing it and one doesn't see anything until one sees its beauty. People see fogs, he says, because poets and painters have taught about them. No one really saw the fogs in London until they were painted, until art invented them. Art never tells us the truth and Wilde is on the side of art more than on the side of depressing truth. Vivian says, 'art, very fortunately, has never once told us the truth'.

So, what to do? Vivian answers: to revive and restore the old art of lying. The light and graceful side of lying can be seen at literary lunches and at afternoon teas but there are many other forms. There is lying in order to gain some immediate personal advantage; there is lying with a moral purpose – in order to procure some good perhaps; there is lying for the sake of the improvement of the young, as the early books of Plato's *Republic* attest; there is lying for the sake of a monthly salary, as in Fleet Street. Indeed, a short primer on lying – 'When to Lie and How' – if brought out in an attractive and not too expensive form would likely command a large sale and would be of real practical service to a lot of deep-thinking people. But the only form of lying that is 'absolutely beyond reproach is lying for its own sake, and the highest development of this is, as we have already pointed out, Lying in Art'. It's more important to love beauty than truth. And when that day dawns, Vivian will be joyous. Facts will be discredited, truth will be found mourning over her fetters, and the wonder of romance will return to a world full of realism. 'Out of the sea will rise Behemoth and Leviathan,' as they said on the maps of old when books of geography were actually readable and dragons 'will wander about the waste places, and the phoenix will soar from her nest of fire into the air', but before all this comes to pass we must cultivate the lost art of lying. Cyril, at the conclusion of this conversation, is convinced and says that we must cultivate it at once. The matter is pressing.

Wilde here reveals the loveliness of lying and ends with the famous declaration and definition of lying as 'the telling of beautiful untrue things' – this being for him the proper end and aim of all art.

Eyes for Lies

Wilde lied in the courtroom and was himself lied to as he looked into the eyes of those rent boys whose bodies he purchased and coveted. Conversely, there are some people who have 'eyes for lies'.

In a research project called The Wizards Project, a 'truth wizard' is a person who has the ability to detect a lie with an 80 per cent or higher rate of accuracy. This would be an amazing accomplishment by any standards. Two scientists conducted the experiment and identified only 50 people as Truth Wizards (what about Lying Witches?) after testing 200,000 people from all walks of life, from students to the Secret Service, from salesmen to sheriffs, from attorneys to arbitrators, from farmers to the FBI. Psychiatrists and law enforcement officers showed no more aptitude than college students, though the Secret Service agents were the most skilled in detecting deceit. Truth Wizards are especially attuned to nuances of facial expression, body language, ways of talking and they spot these micro-expressions which give us away. The TV series *Lie to Me* is based on the work of these researchers. However, most of the time we are taken in by lying eyes as we are held hostage by the sometimes lethal even if lovely look, just as

Wilde was. 'If you love me, you'd lie to me.' 'I've eyes only for you.' But love is blind, just as beauty besots – love wears blinders. Love's a blinder. When do we lie with our eyes? When we blink excessively or not at all. 'Love the way you lie' (Eminem).

• •

'The tongue may hide the truth but the eyes – never!' – Mikhail Bulgakov,
The Master and Margarita

• •

Leading Questions, Lying Answers

And what comes out of our mouths? Within any scenario or situation where dualistic answers such as 'yes/no', 'black/white', are always given, a person whom we know is consistently lying would paradoxically be a source of truth. This is the paradox of lying.

Some questions are more likely to elicit the truth than others. 'When was the last time you smoked some hash?' (a leading question) is more likely to get a truthful answer than, 'Do you smoke hash?' There is no such thing, thank God, as a truth serum. That doesn't mean we don't get anxious when we lie and give ourselves away. 'One may sometimes tell a lie, but the grimace that accompanies it tells the truth' (Nietzsche). We want to get caught out, unconsciously. In relation to biology, the brain may be a perjurer but the body gives the brain away. Think of the technology of the lie detector test, of the polygraph and galvanic skin response. The polygraph shows up the lie in the outpourings of the neuro-hormones. To lie well requires that we don't care too much about getting caught out.

In conversations there is a widespread belief that we can catch people out by closely observing which direction they tilt their heads and look with their eyes. However, according to the most recent scientific experiments, there is no validity to the assertion made by many proponents of Neuro-Linguistic Programming (NLP) that certain eye movements (facial clues or 'tells') are reliable indicators of lying, according to which, a person who looks up to their right is lying, while someone looking up to their left is telling the truth. Studies seem not to support this claim. Liars do not exhibit a particular pattern of eye movement. There is no correlation between eye movement and modality of thought. It is true, though, that liars use fewer and more tentative words, such as 'if', 'perhaps', and 'maybe', and blink more.

The four most common lies you will hear: 'I'm fine', 'I love you', 'We will be together forever' and 'You will use Algebra in real life'. If it's true that the average person (whoever that may be) tells four lies a day (according to one account) then we tell 1,460 lies a year, which amounts to a total of 67,600 by the time we reach the age of 60 (doesn't that depend on when we start?).

Moreover, our use of electronic forms of communication facilitates the lie and issues in an increasingly dishonest future. It's much easier to lie in emails, Facebook posts, Twitter comments and mobile texts, etc. because it's quicker, takes less thought and is intended for the public (even if 'friends', which we've never even met, are 'poked') about whom we care very little.

The 'Science of Honesty' study established a link between lying less and improved mental health, as well as more positive results in participants' personal relationships. And according to the Radical Honesty Movement, everyone would be happier if we told the truth more of the time. Lying, they contend, is the primary source of stress, depression and anxiety.

Anxiety Doesn't Lie

The question is: does anxiety lie? Anxiety is the price we pay for the absence of guilt. Anxiety doesn't lie, according to the philosophers and psychoanalysts who have written on this subject. It's the only affect that doesn't deceive. All other emotions, from sorrow to love, are based ultimately on deceit. You can trust your anxiety, however, even if you don't like it. That's the good news.

We certainly get anxious attempting to recall our lies; that's why Algernon Sydney, the seventeenth-century English political theorist, famously said, 'Liars need to have good memories'. Conversely, as Mark Twain recognised:

$$\bullet$$

'If you tell the truth, you don't have to remember anything.'

$$\bullet\bullet\bullet\bullet\bullet\bullet\bullet\bullet\bullet\bullet\bullet\bullet\bullet\bullet\bullet\bullet\bullet\bullet\bullet$$

Just so. But who can tell the truth? We have answered that earlier: the psychotic, but at the price of his sanity.

Men spend most of their time lying to themselves while women spend their time lying to the Other – with the hope of being caught out. But women have the better memory.

And both sexes lie on their Curriculum Vitaes. CVs read like the fairytales of the world – does anyone really not lie on their *résumés*?

When given an unwelcome gift, I think both men and women find it particularly difficult to lie. One can say, though, and mean it: 'I can't begin to tell you what I think of it!' Women are more likely to 'self-gift' than men.

Lying Cretans

There is paradox at the heart of love too, for in love, as Jacques Lacan, Freud's French follower, tells us, we give what we don't have (our whole self) to someone who doesn't want it (they want part-objects such as eyes, lips etc.). But there is also paradox at the heart of logic (for example, a perfectly logically valid syllogism is: 'The Statue of Liberty is in Madrid. Madrid is in Spain. Therefore, the Statue of Liberty is in Spain.' But it just so happens, in reality, that the Statue of Liberty is in New York) and paradox at the heart of our lies/truth-telling too. Logic lies.

There is what is known as the Liar's Paradox (originally devised in the fourth century BC by Eubulides who said: 'A man says that he's lying. Is what he says true or false?'). Epimenides, a Cretan, reportedly said: 'The Cretans are always liars.' Is he lying when he says this? The statement is false as long as there exists at least one Cretan who has told the truth at least once. Another example of a 'Liar's Paradox' in logic is the statement, 'This statement is false'. If 'This sentence is false' is true, then it is false, which would in turn mean that it's actually true but this would mean that it's false, etc. Epimenides, a Cretan, asserts that, 'All Cretans are liars', as we said above. If he is telling the truth, then he is lying. This is like when I say the following: 'What I am now saying is false' – here the intention to deceive is set aside. I will spare you any detailed discussion about principles of bivalence, laws of the excluded middle, paraconsistent logic, situational semantics, dialetheism, and Tarski's and Gödel's mathematical theorems, mainly because I don't know any of them myself, and just tell you that, aside from these logical non-Cretans, I personally know many lying, non-logical cretins.

1: The sentence printed below is false.

2: The sentence written above is true.

If the second sentence is true, then the first is true; but if the first is true, the second is false. I feel I'm going round in circles. You too?

The Liar's Paradox is best summed up by Ludwig Wittgenstein, himself a logician, thus:

● ●

'If a man says "I am lying" we say that it follows that he is not lying, from which it follows that he is lying and so on. Well, so what? You can go on like that until you are black in the face.'

● ●

Or blue in the face, for that matter.

Wittgenstein elaborated the notion of 'language games', each with its own set of rules; so the 'truth' is determined by those rules. Lying would be equivalent to a soccer player picking up the ball and running with it. However, if that game were rugby that would be 'truthful' behaviour. Wittgenstein marvelled at the fact that lying comes so easily to us and recalls how at the age of eight he was struck by the question: why speak the truth if there is something to be gained by telling a lie? He still felt lying to have a harmful effect on one. In *Culture and Value*, Wittgenstein writes:

• •

'Often, it is only very slightly more disagreeable to tell the truth than to lie; about as difficult as drinking bitter rather than sweet coffee; and yet I still have a strong inclination to lie.'

• •

Furthermore, not all true propositions can be proved. When someone says to you, 'I always lie', you can trust them! It was a lie that I always lie. So I don't always lie. 'No, it's all lies.' But the true liar may be bluffing when he says this. In this way, I am deceiving you. By so doing, I am telling the truth. Freud's Jewish joke comes to mind (earlier I gave another version of it):

• •

'Two Jews met in a railway carriage in
Galicia. "Where are you going?" asked one.
"To Cracow," was the answer. "What a liar
you are!" broke out the other. "If you say
you're going to Cracow, you want me to
believe you're going to Lemberg. But I know
that in fact you're going to Cracow.
So why are you lying to me?".'

• •

Since, according to Freud, there are no indications
of reality in the unconscious, we cannot distinguish between truth and fiction.

Freud spent a lot of his time analysing 'hysterics'. In
1866, Jules Falret, the French doctor, wrote: 'The life of
the hysteric is one perpetual lie.' However, in October
1910 at a meeting of the Vienna Psychoanalytic Society,
Freud intervened when Alfred Adler, the psychologist,
spoke on hysterical lying. The Minutes tell us Freud
said the following: 'The mendacity of hysterics calls
to mind the old paradox of the Cretan: if a hysterical
woman asserts that she has lied, it may be precisely this
assertion that is a lie.'

But lies can be analysed. Freud analysed little Hans'
lies (the five-year-old phobic); they were anything but
meaningless. However, analysis is not for everyone. For
one thing it costs a lot and requires a lot of investment –

financial, emotional, etc. It is a psychoanalytic dictum/ truism that money never lies.

Truth is cheerless; lying is creative. There is the liar and then there is the bullshitter. 'Don't bullshit a bullshitter.' His speech is empty; it is idle. But the Freudian lesson here is that we need to take lies seriously; they are an indication of powerful passions, of deep desires. So much goes on in our unconscious; lies that dare not speak their name. Freud had this to say about that:

• •

'There are countless civilized people who would shrink from murder or incest but who do not deny themselves the satisfaction of their avarice, their aggressive urges or their sexual lusts, and who do not hesitate to injure other people by lies, fraud and calumny.'

• • • • • • • • • • •

Our lying dreams give us away. Also, protestations: 'I'm telling you the truth' (said in a slightly shrill voice); this means, if we follow Freud's logic in his article, 'Negation', that the person is lying. Such is the language of lies. Which one of us when stopped by the police behaves as if we were not guilty? We are all guilty of something. Isn't the person who doesn't lie the ultimate moral monster? All speech is destined to deceive and that's why we enjoy talking so much. The French philosopher, Jean-Jacques Rousseau, in his *Reveries*, asserts:

• •

'I have often made up stories, but very rarely told lies.'

• • • • • • • • • • • • • • • •

A Tale of Three

Here's another brain teaser: three goddesses were sitting in an old Indian temple. Their names are Truth (who always tells the truth), Lie (who always lies) and Wisdom (who sometimes lies). A visitor asks the one on the left, 'Who is sitting next to you?' 'Truth,' she answered. Then he asks the one in the middle, 'Who are you?' 'Wisdom,' is the response. Lastly, he asks the one on the right, 'Who is your neighbour?' 'Lie,' she replies. And then it became clear who is who. Can you work it out? Write down all the combinations of orientation and rule them out one by one. Let T = Truth, W = Wisdom and L = Lie. Thus:

TWL: Truth would not lie about Wisdom's position

TLW: Truth would not lie about Lie's position

LTW: Lie would lie about Truth's position

LWT: Truth would not lie about Wisdom's position

WTL: Truth would not lie about her own position.

So, it must be: WLT: Wisdom, Lie, Truth, in that order. To put it another way, Truth is neither the one on the left nor the middle since she won't lie about who is beside her or who she is. Therefore, she is on the right side and she was telling the truth that Lie was sitting beside her in the middle, which leaves Wisdom on the left.

Above, Wisdom sometimes lies, we are told. So does this mean that wisdom dictates that we sometimes lie and sometimes tell the truth? It would seem logical that this is true but four thinkers stand out in the history of Western thought for their strict condemnations of all forms of lying. They are St. Augustine, St. Thomas Aquinas, Michel de Montaigne and Immanuel Kant. Despite their different philosophies, they had that in common – their detestation of all forms of lying. They held that there are no circumstances whatsoever in which one may lie. One must be murdered or tortured rather than lie. Lying, they thought, is a perversion, one that undermines trust in society. (Some might say that their twisted logic, on this subject at any rate, is a perversion.) Anyway, let's see what they have to say on the subject.

Against Lying

St. Augustine

St. Augustine, who condemned all lying (even the 'well meant lie') except jocose lies (not a real lie since there is lack of intention to deceive), outlined a taxonomy of lies in two books: *De Mendacio (On Lying)* and *Contra Mendacio (Against Lying)*. In Chapter Fourteen of the former work he divides lies into eight categories:

1. Lies told in religious teaching (these are deadly lies and must be shunned)

2. Lies that harm or injure others unjustly

3. Lies that are beneficial to one person but harm another

4. Lies told solely for the pleasure of lying (the 'real lie')

5 Lies told from a desire to 'please others in smooth discourse'

6. Lies that harm no one but benefit some person

7. Lies that harm no one and that save someone's life

8. Lies that harm no one and that save someone's 'purity'.

According to Augustine, it is better to err by an excessive regard for the truth and by an equally emphatic rejection of falsehood. A lie is pernicious since it has as its objective the deliberate desire to deceive. It's a kind of false faith. Some people tell what is false without the intention of deceiving, while others tell what is true in order to deceive. A lie is a false statement and Augustine does not condone or sanction any form of lying, even if it secures the salvation of another, for 'the good never lie'. He goes so far as to say that one's 'eternal life is lost by lying'. Telling lies harms those who tell them. So, we should not only not lie but not even want to lie. Lying is never morally justified is the verdict of this stern Bishop of Hippo. Lying is a sin and the motive of the liar determines the gravity of the lie (it makes a difference, he contends, for what reason, to what end and with what intention lying is performed). However, all lies are to be detested 'uniformly'. To those who say that some lies are just or justifiable, Augustine replies then we would have to say that there are some just sins and that, consequently, some things that are unjust are just. Ultimately, lies should be either avoided altogether or be confessed in penitence.

St. Thomas Aquinas

Following Saints Augustine and Aquinas, Catholic moral theologians tend to distinguish between 1) injurious (hurtful) lies, 2) officious lies, and 3) jocose lies. Jocose lies are told for the purpose of amusement – they are said merely in joke and so cannot be considered lies. An officious lie is a white lie, such that it does nobody any injury – it's a lie of excuse. An injurious lies does harm. Two schools of thought on this vexed moral question have arisen as regards ethical considerations: Aristotle (and following him Augustine, Aquinas and Kant) in his *Ethics* seems to hold that it is never permissible to tell a lie, while Plato, in his *Republic*, is more lenient about lying – he allows doctors and statesmen to lie for the good of their patients and citizens. Thus, the lawfulness of the lie of necessity. But some Catholic theologians would insist that white lies are apt to prepare the way for others of a darker hue: white leading to scarlet, so. Church Fathers such as Origen, St. John Chrysostom and Cassian followed Plato's lead on lies. The Western Church has, in the main, adopted the Augustinian position that it is never lawful to lie. Innocent III interpreted Scripture as forbidding us to lie even to save a person's life.

For Thomas Aquinas, lying is opposed to the virtue of veracity. Truth consists in a correspondence between the thing signified and the signification of it. The essence of a lie is the want of right moral order (hence the employment of the word 'disorder'). According to Aquinas, the lie has harmful consequences for society. They can affect the rights and reputations of others; friendship can even suffer from jocose lying. Promiscuous lying leads to mistrust, suspicion and loss of confidence.

Moreover, when a habit for telling lies has been formed it is practically impossible to undo. For Thomas, we are never justified in telling a lie because the end never justifies the means (we may not do evil so that good may come). So (to take an example from Augustine) if silence would be equivalent to giving a sick man unwelcome news that would kill him, it is better that the body of the sick man should perish rather than the soul of the liar. Or, to take another example, if a man is hiding in your house and his life is sought by murderers and they come and ask you if he is in the house, you may say you know where he is but will not tell; you may not deny that he is there (Kant cites a similar example as we shall see). The lie possesses intrinsic malice. Later, some Schoolmen would endorse 'mental reservations' and 'equivocations' in speech. So the Thomistic answer to the classification of lies is as follows: hurtful lies are mortal sins; officious and jocose lies are venial sins. Are you a mortal or venial sinner, dear reader?

Michel de Montaigne

In 1572, Michel de Montaigne penned his 'assays' and he has some strict things to say on lying, especially in his essay entitled 'On Giving the Lie'. 'The first sign of corrupt morals is the banishing of truth,' he writes in his famous *Essays*. Lying corrupts morals. Montaigne would concur with Pindar's view that being truthful is the beginning of any great virtue. And Plato required this of the Governor in his *Republic*. Montaigne, himself

French, opines that lying has become, not just a vice for the French but a figure of speech. For Montaigne, the lie is the most accursed vice: 'the ultimate verbal insult to accuse us of lying'. Montaigne feels it is cowardly to deny one's word, that is to say, to lie. He talks about the horror and vileness and disorderliness of lies and labels it a 'villein's vice'. If we lie, society cannot be held together and nor can we. Montaigne opines:

• •

**'When words deceive us, it breaks
all intercourse and loosens
the bonds of our polity.'**

• • • • • • • • • • • • • • • • • • • •

To lie is *mentiri* in Latin. To tell an untruth is to say something false, which one thinks to be true. This is different, so, from lying. Many people have recognised the intimate connection between memory and lying, in that one has to have a good memory to lie. This was first recognised by Quintilian. And according to Montaigne, one can catch out liars by making them tell the same story several times over. Lies so easily slip out of memory. In a section in his *Essays* entitled 'On liars', Montaigne writes:

● ●

'It is only our words which bind us together and make us human. If we realized the horror and weight of lying we would see that it is more worthy of the stake than other crimes. I find that people normally waste time quite inappropriately punishing children for innocent misdemeanours, tormenting them for thoughtless actions which lead nowhere and leave no trace. It seems to me that the only faults which we should rigorously attack as soon as they arise and start to develop are lying and, a little below that, stubbornness. Those faults grow up with the children. Once let the tongue acquire the habit of lying, and it is astonishing how impossible it is to make it give it up.'

● ●

In this respect Montaigne is similar to Augustine who likewise emphasises the damaging and detrimental effects of lying in discourse, as we saw. In his *City of God*, Augustine says that a dog we do know is better company than a man whose language we don't know and that the language of lies is less comprehensible than silence even.

Immanuel Kant

In 'On a Supposed Right to Tell Lies from Benevolent
Motives', the great German philosopher Immanuel Kant
laid it down as a moral principle the duty to speak the
truth no matter what. Truth in utterances is the formal
duty of everyone even if great disadvantage arises from
it. Kant defines a lie as 'an intentionally false declaration towards another man'; it will always cause injury
to another since it vitiates the source of justice. What
comes next is Kant's famous example: if you have, by a
lie, stopped a man from planning a murder, you are le-
gally responsible for all the consequences. If, however,
you strictly adhered to the truth, public justice will find
no fault in you. There will always be, contends Kant, unforeseen consequences. It is possible, he says, that while
you honestly answered 'yes' to the murderer's question
as to whether his intended victim is in his house, the
victim may have gone out unobserved and so not have
come into the way of the murderer and the dastardly
deed would not have been done; whereas if you lied and
said he was not in the house and that he had really gone
out (though unknown to you) so that the murderer met
him as he went and 'executed his purpose' on him, then
you might with justice be accused as the cause of his
death. Kant says if you had spoken the truth as you
knew it, perhaps the murderer while searching for his
enemy in the house might have been caught by some

neighbours arriving on the scene and the deed would have been prevented. Kant is adamant:

• •

'Whoever then tells a lie, however good his intentions may be, must answer for the consequences of it, even before the civil tribunal, and must pay the penalty for them, however unforeseen they may have been; because truthfulness is a duty that must be regarded as the basis of all duties founded on contract, the laws of which would be rendered uncertain and useless if even the least exception to them were admitted. To be truthful (honest) in all declarations is therefore a sacred unconditional command of reason, and not to be limited by any expediency.'

• •

So, for this stringent German philosopher (is there any other type?), truth-telling is an unconditional duty. There you have it. So act in accordance with your duty, not your desire.

Thomas Jefferson, like Kant, felt that lying was always wrong:

• •

**'He who permits himself to tell a lie
once, finds it much easier to do it
a second and third time, till at length
it becomes habitual.'**

• • • • • • • • • • • • • • • • • • •

The falsehood of the tongue leads to the falsehood of the heart.

• •

**'Lying is hateful and accursed vice. We have
no other tie upon one another, but
our word.' – Immanuel Kant**

• •

'A single lie destroys a whole reputation for integrity' (Balthasar Gracian, Spanish Jesuit), unless of course the lie is motivated by integrity in the first place. As Baruch Spinoza, the Dutch philosopher, tells us: men govern nothing with greater difficulty than their tongues, as we bear false witness. That said, we moderate our desires quicker than our words.

The Truth in the Lie

B ut those of us who are not saints, German philoso-phers, or American presidents tend both to lie and tell the truth as the situation dictates, distinguishing between little and big lies, noble and ignoble ones. Isn't wisdom precisely the capacity to do so? Only the 'pervert' (understood not as a stigma but as a clinical category) separates Truth from Lies. What, though, does he miss in thus separating the two? The truth of the lie itself – the truth that is contained and delivered in the very act of lying. The truth resonates in the lie. Shakespeare's play, *All's Well that Ends Well*, is all about the entanglements of truth and lies. The lie can reveal the truth about the person.

In his book, *The Doctor and the Soul*, Viktor Frankl, the Austrian psychiatrist, concentration camp survivor and founder of logotherapy, opines that honesty is paradoxical, that 'one can lie with truth and, on the other hand, tell the truth with a lie – even make something true by a lie'. He gives the example of a doctor who takes the patient's blood pressure and finds it high. The patient asks him to tell him the reading. But if the doctor does so the patient will be so alarmed and agitated that his blood pressure will rise even higher than it already is. If the doctor does not tell him the truth but gives him a false reading in order to reassure him his blood pressure may drop so that in the end the sham lie will be an exact statement.

Knowledge is factual; it is objective. Truth, though, is subjective. One can lie in the guise of truth. This is what men are doing when, in statements that are factually entirely accurate they conceal or deny their real desire. One can also tell the truth in the guise of a lie. This is what women do; their slips of the tongue betray their true desire. We need to spell this out in some detail. But before we do, let me ask the question: is there such a thing as the 'Right to Lie'?

The Right to Lie?

Rights at their core are 'Rights to Violate', ... just as law is the cause of crime (I'm being a bit facetious). Freedom of religious belief is the right to worship false gods. The right to possess private property is the right to steal. And Freedom of the Press and the Free Expression of Opinion is the right to lie. So it would seem that men and women possess the right to lie; the question is, who does so more successfully? Much will depend on whether we want to get caught out, consciously or unconsciously.

The Successful Lie

To lie successfully one needs to insert some truth into the lie. 'If you wish to strengthen a lie, mix a little truth in with it,' *The Zohar* (the rabbinic work on Jewish mysticism) tells us. Similarly, Iris Murdoch, the Irish philosopher, observes: 'We have to mix a little falsehood into truth to make it plausible.' It's a surer way of not getting found out – if that's what you really want.

Benjamin Disraeli famously said that there were three kinds of lies: lies, damned lies, and statistics. We can manipulate the truth so that it becomes a lie, so that the line between lies and truth-telling becomes blurred, eclipsed, as politicians and propagandists know only too well. With regards to lawyers, isn't it interesting to note that there is a homophony between 'lawyer' and 'liar'?

The distinction between lies and truth is not at all clear-cut, despite the protestations of Augustine, Aquinas and Kant to the contrary. Most of us mix fact with fiction, fantasy and falsehood with lies and truth, as Walter Mitty meets Pinocchio. At times, all our noses grow. And there are some people who have a nose for lies; they can sniff it out and smell a lie a mile away.

As Dr. Lecter (Hannibal the cannibal) says to Clarice: 'Don't lie or I'll know.' He was psychotic of course, wasn't he? Mad or bad?

• •

'Falsehood is so easy, truth so difficult.... Examine your words well, and you will find that even when you have no motive to be false, it is a very hard thing to say the exact truth, even about your own immediate feelings – much harder than to say something fine about them which is not the exact truth.' — George Eliot, *Adam Bede*

• •

Needing Lies

T.S. Eliot, the American-British poet, once said that man can't bear too much reality; Freud said it too. Well, we can't bear too much truth either. Look what happens in the film *Liar Liar* when Jim Carey tells the truth: chaos and social anarchy ensue. Roger Scruton, the British philosopher, expressed it well:

● ●

**'The human world flourishes best
when refreshed by falsehood.'**

● ●

Truth is sometimes stranger than fiction but we need some fictions to live by, as the philosopher David Hume recognised. We need lies in order to live with the awful, painful, hurtful, truthful reality that is life. Some people, though, desperately hold on to a belief system, to take an example, even when they know it's false; it gives them a sense of comfort and security. We recall Nietzsche's quip that convictions are more dangerous foes of truth than lies. Be wary of the person who seems so sure.

Nietzsche, for whom all morality is based on lies, had warned us to beware of the good and their 'noble lies', but Plato endorsed the 'noble lie' (lying for good reason). And I do too, against the above thinkers. We saw how Kant (with whom I 'can't' agree – sorry, couldn't resist) forbade lying even in the case of a murderer asking us where we buried the axe-knife. It just shows you that incredibly intelligent people can be really rather stupid. There can be integrity in lying surely, depending on one's motivations? Moral lying, so. Whatever about integrity in lying, there can also be an enjoyment, a *jouissance* (painful pleasure), in lying.

Enjoying Lying

We enjoy exaggerating stories, embellishing events, as we engage in hysterical hyperbole. 'A mixture of a lie doth ever add pleasure' (Montaigne). Too true. Remember the last time you exaggerated a story for the pleasure of your friends? 'You should have been there! There were ten of them and I got the biggest one down and the rest ran away' or 'It was the largest spider I have ever seen in the shower'. The story grows wings. There is a thin line between exaggeration and lying, between lying to ourselves and being deluded.

Henry James, the novelist brother of the philosopher William James, in a short story, 'The Liar', written after meeting a man who told tall tales at a dinner party recounts a story about compulsive but well-intentioned social liars. The narrator becomes aware that his dinner companion is caught in a compulsion to lie; referring to this lying Colonel Capadose, Sir David Ashmore, the master of the house, says: 'He'll lie about the time of day, about the name of his hatter.' There is no harm in the hapless Colonel, however. 'He doesn't steal or cheat nor gamble nor drink; he's very kind – he sticks to his wife, is fond of his children. He simply can't give you a straight answer.'

We speak the words we think the other wants to hear. But people hear what they want to hear. You lie because you don't want to tell them what they need to hear. With drink, we relish the truth more.

• •

'Carlyle said "a lie cannot live". It shows that he did not know how to tell them.' – Mark Twain

• • • • • • • • • • • • • • •

Lies, Drink and Guilt

We tell less lies with drink on us. But lying, as Steven Soderbergh, the screenwriter of *Sex, Lies and Videotape*, tells us, 'is like alcoholism – you are always recovering'. I am a recovering liar. Jokes, like alcohol, excuse and encourage the lie and mitigate the guilt so the unsaid may be spoken.

Lying brings about its own punishment – the punishment of guilt. 'Conscience doth make cowards of us all' (Shakespeare). Also this:

• •

**'The liar's punishment is that they
cannot believe anybody else.'
– George Bernard Shaw**

• • • • • • • • • • • • • • • • • • •

His punishment perhaps, but also his pleasure. (Some people will only commit a crime provided they get punished.) But between men and women, who lies best?

The Best Liar

In a sentence: the best liar is the one who has nothing to lose. 'No one lies so boldly as the man who is indifferent' (Nietzsche). On one interpretation, freedom is just another word for having nothing left to lose – at least that's what Kris Kristofferson tells us.

• •

'I'm the most terrific liar you ever saw in your life. It's awful. If I'm on my way to the store to buy a magazine, even, and somebody asks me where I'm going, I'm liable to say I'm going to the opera. It's terrible.'
— J.D. Salinger, *The Catcher in the Rye*

• •

Lying in Bed

Men and women both lie in bed and, as I have said in another book, there's always at least four lovers/liars in every bed, four-poster or otherwise. 'I love you. I can't live without you. You are my everything.' We lie in the arms of our lovers. The opposite of a lie? Saying what you like. Is lying a defence against desire? What is the lie of the land?

Julian Barnes, the English novelist, in his *A History of the World in 10½ Chapters*, has this to say about lovers lying in bed:

• •

'Have you ever told so much truth as when you were first in love? Have you ever seen the world so clearly? Love makes us see the truth, makes it our duty to tell the truth. Lying in bed: listen to the undertow of warning in that phrase. Lying in bed, we tell the truth: it sounds like a paradoxical sentence from a first-year philosophy primer. But it's more (and less) than that: a description of moral duty.'

• •

Lying in Bed

And Dorothy Parker, the American poet and satirist, writes:

● ●

'By the time you say you're his,
Shivering and sighing
And he vows his passion is
Infinite, undying –
Lady, make note of this:
One of you is lying.'

● ● ● ● ● ● ● ● ● ● ● ● ● ● ● ● ●

Lying versus Deceiving

Lying is an action but lying can never describe the whole situation or scenario. Deception, by contrast, pertains to the dynamics of lying. In deception there is the liar and the lied to but more than this. Lying is commonly regarded as binary, but the presence of the unconscious complicates matters; deception is more general – there is more going on. A lie is something you tell – it covers up, camouflages. A deception is something you perform, in which you participate. Deception is bigger than the individuals involved. You can deceive someone without there being a truth to deceive about. The mechanics of the *déjà vu* phenomenon bring out the differences well. A *déjà vu* experience is one of a glitch in perception; it's a trick being played out, enacted. I see a glass once; the mind, however, tricks me into thinking that I have seen it twice. That is deception, a 'lie', if you like, without a liar. But the mind hasn't lied to you –that's the thing; the 'reality' is that you have seen it twice. Deception uses the truth but not in the way a lie does. Deception is indebted to the truth whereas (in traditional terms) a lie uses truth only to support itself as a negation. Deception certainly doesn't necessitate the presence of a (guilty) person/party. So if we say something like 'men lie, women deceive', we mean 'deceive' colloquially (as I do in this book), suggesting a certain sneakiness absent in 'straight'-forward male lying because women are more complex creatures than men. With women's lies there is always more happening. It is this 'more' (the plus factor) that is absent in the lying ways of (mere) men.

Truth is intimately tied up with deception, as I have said, as is hypocrisy, which always includes deception. A hypocrite is a liar who doesn't know he's a liar. Deception and lies are not the opposite of truth; on the contrary, they are inscribed in the text of truth. Putting it another way, there is truth in deception. My writing here in this study, in search of truth, is 'error taking flight in deception and recaptured by mistake' (Lacan). If the unconscious is structured like a language (contested by non-Lacanians), truth is structured like a fiction.

Now, before we see how exactly it is that men and women lie differently, we need to establish the differences, in general, between the sexes, and so I go, more tentatively than tenaciously, where angels fear to tread.

Some Differences between Men and Women

Acaveat to begin with: when I say 'men are such and such' or 'women are this and that', please, dear reader, insert a mental 'most' before such sentences, as in 'most men' or 'most women', because there are exceptions. I'm speaking in generalities; finesse is for footnotes. Furthermore, sometimes one has to over hit the mark in order to hit the mark. As the French philosopher Jacques Derrida once remarked, in philosophy, truth is hyperbole. What follows below and in the following section are my sometimes tongue-in-cheek observations – please don't take them too literally – as well as my interpretations of Lacanian theory, on which I freely draw. It is one perspective, a point of view, not facts or the Truth. Feel free to accept or remorselessly reject the reflections offered. With this in mind, let's just jump into this controversial and sometimes acrimonious debate (please, no hate mail/male). Here, as always, the reader is the jury and must judge on the reasonableness (or otherwise) of my contentions/convictions that have been partially formed by French psychoanalytical insights.

● ●

'Men lie the most, women tell the biggest lies.' — Chris Rock

● ●

Men and women are very different beings. Most men are obsessionals, while most women are hysterics (what is meant by this is conveyed below). Men are more straightforward, more blunt than women, while women are more manipulative than men. Men make friends easier than women, probably because most of them remain more superficial. Men are more loyal, but only because they are less overtly emotionally invested. Women are moodier. Their personalities change more (biologically); they also posses more depth than men (psychologically). Men are more constant, more consistent, more stubborn. Women are more complex creatures and, therefore, less predictable. One generally knows where one stands with a man (if one is a man); with women things aren't so clear (if one is a man).

Women need to be needed. Men are more able to be alone; they're more independent. Some men are more in touch with their feminine side (the metrosexual with his 'anima' and 'bromances') than other males of the species, just as some women are more in touch with their masculine sides (their so-called 'animus'). Women test men a lot of the time; they up the ante by pushing the boundaries just to see how far they can go and how much they can get away with. By so doing, they play a dangerous game. In this way, men may be more mistreated than women. Women can emasculate men while men may, as a result, become hen-pecked or cuckolded or turn into wife-beaters.

Women have a higher EQ than men, while men have a higher IQ (though most of these intelligence tests are written and measured by men, it has to be said). Of course, in all what I am saying, one has to take into account age, class, economics, cultural considerations and recent significant shifts in social roles, and these few pages do not admit of such subtleties. I reiterate: I am painting in broad brushstrokes. And, needless to say, parenthood changes nearly everything, even if pro-creative sex is narcissistic.

Men are plagued by thoughts in their mind. Women are plagued by pains in their bodies. Men engage in compulsive rituals, women in somatic symptoms. With regards to sex and sexuality, men react with guilt and aversion, women with disgust and revulsion. Often this is repressed. Unconsciously, neither sex really likes sex. Women seek to discover what the desire of the other person is in order to become that desired object. Women are looking for the Master, that is, someone imbued with knowledge, wealth, status or power. Both sexes ask the philosophical question: 'What am I?' However, women's primary question is: 'Am I a man or a woman?'

whereas men's is: 'Am I dead or alive?' (to be explained below).

• •

**'Don't cry, I'm sorry to have deceived you
so much, but that's how life is.'
— Vladimir Nabokov, *Lolita***

• •

Men feel that they are only really alive when they are consciously thinking and should they lapse into fantasy or stop thinking, for example, during orgasm, men lose any conviction of being. Men believe they are Masters of their own fate; as beings who are whole and complete and in need of no Other to fill up their lack, which they deny having in the first place. Men fiercely refuse to see themselves as dependent on anyone other than themselves. That's just part of their problem. They transform their partner into a mother figure, as a provider of maternal love. Men tend to create two classes of women: the Madonna and the whore – truthful prudes or lying sluts. They may have sex with the latter but they tend to marry the former. For men, all partners are pretty much the same. That's why they get over failed relationships quicker than women. For women (women, not girls), there's no such thing as an unwanted pregnancy; most women get pregnant on purpose.

Women, in contrast to men, over-emphasise the other person, making themselves into the object of the other person's desire so as to master it. I said above that women seek a Master, yes, they seek a Master (he who is unable not to know everything) to master (it's always on their terms). Feminists are half-right and half-wrong. There is a war between the sexes but there is also a war between men and men and women and women. There's no equality between men and women. Women don't want to be equal to men – they want to be treated better than men. Deservedly so.

The Other whom the woman desires is desired but when and how the woman sees fit. She orchestrates things in such a way as to ensure that the other person's desire remains unsatisfied leaving her a permanent place as 'object'. Woman's desire is characterised by a desire for an unsatisfied desire and that's why women are unhappier than men in matters of love. So much is invested in the Other without whom they feel they don't exist ('You are my all; you are my everything'). For women it's a case of 'too much being not enough', whereas for men it's a case of even a little being a lot. For this reason women are more jealous than men (jealousy is triadic) while men are more envious than women (envy is dyadic).

Men's desire is impossible rather than unsatisfied because they neutralise their partner so they don't have to consider themselves dependent on her, on her desire for them in any way. Men desire what is unattainable. While having sex men tend to fantasise that they are with someone else, thereby negating the importance of the actual person they are with. The closer men get to fulfilling their desire the more the other person takes precedence over him, eclipsing him, and men can't tolerate this. To avoid it, a typical male strategy is to fall in love with someone who is utterly and completely inaccessible, or to set standards for potential lovers that are so strict or stringent that no one can possibly live up to them. Men demand perfection, mainly from themselves (of course, perfection is not possible). Men have a common fantasy of being seduced by a woman without their active involvement (hence his predilection and penchant for masturbation).

Women, by contrast, desire their male partner; they desire them as if they were them, as if they were men. Women often create love triangles centred on one man and indeed thrive on these. Women ask: 'Who do you say I am?' They are always trying to find out who they are but via the Other – 'What about me? What am I like?' Bette Midler said in a film: 'Enough about me. What about you? What do you think about me?' Women find men's sexual satisfaction distasteful and try to avoid becoming the object on which men get off. They want to be the cause of men's love not their lust. When having sex, women are inclined to imagine that some other man is in bed with her, that she is somewhere else or someone else, or that he is a different man. If men block out the woman present to make her absent, women are mentally somewhere else during sex. Women can't find sexual satisfaction and love in the same relationship. So there is no such thing as harmonious sexual relations; they don't work – not at the level of the drives, anyway. There is no sexual rapport but that's a good thing. It means men and women will keep having sex under the erroneous assumption that they will become whole and lack nothing. Women, especially, want to become one with the other person but there is no such thing as unity at the level of love. Men and women are two not one. Fantasy sustains both sexes. Furthermore, there is no such person as Mr Right or the perfect partner; there are only 'good enough others', but that is never enough for women, hence their perpetual dissatisfaction in love relations. Men, for their part, are more defensive, more distant and, as a consequence, they get hurt less and 'move on' more easily, as I said. In this respect, men are more like cats, women more like dogs.

Women tend to live in the past more than men – they view photographs and photograph albums more and look at pictures more; they 'suffer from reminiscences' (Freud) and associative memories. Men live more for the future. Men are attentive to their own needs. Women are more attentive to what the other person wants (though, it has to be said, via her). Men would really rather forget the Other. Women look (up) to the Other to fill their lack ('I can only be happy with him'). Women's desire is an insatiable appetite; women always want more. It is a 'wanting more' that is problematic for men because men just can't (or won't) give it. Psychologically, men and women appear to each other as a different species. 'Men are from Mars; women are from Venus,' as the saying goes.

• •

'"Was it necessary to tell me that you wanted nothing in the world but me?" The corners of his mouth drooped peevishly. "Oh, my dear, it's rather hard to take quite literally the things a man says when he's in love with you." "Didn't you mean them?" "At the moment."' — W. Somerset Maugham, *The Painted Veil*

• • • • • • • • • • • • • •

When angry, women will hurl hysterical abuse at men: 'Without me, you'd be nothing.' They keep on challenging, defiant and demanding. Such is their feminine ferocity. Because women are alienated from their own desire (by prioritising the desire of the Other at the expense of their own which they subordinate) they often portray themselves as victims – sacrificial lambs – ready to sacrifice everything for their idealised Other. But ultimately she will come to resent the man who puts her in this position and her love can quickly change to hate. A woman scorned is as lethal as a tarantula ('hell hath no fury like a woman scorned,' as Shakespeare famously observed). Women are more cunning than men because (they believe) they have so much to lose, they will fight accordingly for what they want and feel is theirs by right (understandably).

Women tend to lament that they haven't been loved enough by the Other (be it the mother in childhood or the present partner who could do more for her). Women feel they haven't received the full evidence of this love. Men tend to think they have been loved too much. Women tend to stage a show, to show themselves off to the Other whom they are intent on having. They offer themselves up to the gaze of the Other as ideal object of desire. They want to fascinate the Other and appear as brilliant and beautiful. But the more they do this the more men close down; it is all just too much. Women, so, are mistresses at not getting what they want. Women want to be permanently reassured. Men feel they simply can't give women what they want and they relapse into their solitary world, exhausted, assuming that they even give a damn in the first place. Women vampirise men. For women, love is fusional cannibalism ('I could just eat him up'). For men, love is lack. If men are looking for their mothers in women, women are looking for their fathers in men.

Women, in anger, throw fits of rage; their emotional outbursts experienced as being caused by the other person who is making them so unhappy ('you made me like this; it's your fault'). Men, when angry, tend to withdraw in silence. Women are architects, however, of their own misfortune. Women want the argument to clear the air; men want to flee such an unpleasantry and forget – hence their tendency to solitary escape: 'I just need my space' – words women hate to hear. Men are more moral (they do their duty) while women are more ethical (they act more from desire).

. . . .

'The girl was grateful to the young man for every bit of flattery; she wanted to linger for a moment in its warmth and so she said, "You're very good at lying." "Do I look like a liar?" "You look like you enjoy lying to women," said the girl, and into her words there crept unawares a touch of the old anxiety, because she really did believe that her young man enjoyed lying to women.'
— Milan Kundera, *Laughable Loves*

. . . .

Women talk more than men. Women are more oral (needy and narcissistic) while men are more anal (retentive and rigid). Men keep things to themselves. Women are more demanding of others. Men feel they have a duty to endure everything. Men are more rivalrous and competitive (the trophy wife). They try constantly to take the place of the father but men are held captive to the mother. Men are more sarcastic than women; they are also more stubborn and more overtly controlling, and maintain more self-control than women. Men's humour borders on derision. Men desire (self) control. They seldom get it with women. Theirs is the illusion of mastery. Men give very little away so they lose nothing. Men would prefer if women didn't demand so much because in their demand is their desire.

Men's sexuality is simple in that it goes through three stages: erection, ejaculation, temporary impotence. So, one man is all men. Women's sexuality is multiple, non-measurable, maybe even mystical, certainly more complicated than men's. Men's sexuality is that of the masturbator. For men, sex is mostly masturbation with a real partner (Woody Allen: 'Don't knock masturbation, it's sex with someone I love'). Men desire that the Other be dead in relation to desire (which they experience as demand). Men and women complement each other – but only at the level of their symptoms.

Men barter marriage for sex; women barter sex for marriage. Men 'have sex' while women 'make love'. Men can separate these two in a way women can't. For men, two's a crowd; for women, three's a couple. If women are bitches in love, men are bastards in heat. Men parade (they are cocky) just as women masquerade (wear more masks). Men are pimps; women are prostitutes. Men hear but don't listen; women listen but don't hear. Listening, however, is a rarely practised art-form. A man's question is articulated in terms of 'how' – how to be a man. A woman's question concerns 'what' – what does it mean to be a woman. Women want to be accepted and admired; men want to be envied. Women want relationships (love); men want respect (loyalty). Men are more logical ('left-brained'), while women are more loving ('right-brained'). What do men desire? Part-objects: some just want a safe place to put their penis. What do women want? Their partner: the whole world. Him entire – everything, so. The woman does not really exist for man as a real subject but only as a fantasy object. Woman cannot function sexually as woman but only as mother. The woman doesn't exist, just as the father is always uncertain.

When in surveys relating to infidelity women are asked if they would prefer their partner to make love with someone else and think about them, the majority of women said that they would prefer if their partner slept with another woman while thinking of them. Men, on the contrary, said they would prefer if their partner slept with them while thinking of another man. Women, it would seem, want the love of the man (not his body). Women, by remaining (physically) faithful to a man, ultimately deceives him, because what she loves is a phantom, a ghost.

Antoine Tudal, the French director, philosophised thus:

• •

'Between man and love, there is woman.
Between man and woman, there is a world.
Between man and the world, there is a wall.'

• •

Madame de Staël, the Swiss writer, for her part, proclaimed:

• •

'The desire of the man is for the
woman. The desire of the woman
is for the desire of the man.'

• •

How Men and Women Lie in Different Ways

Now we come to address what is our central concern – how men and women lie. In lying, men are more direct while women are more devious (which can be taken as a compliment!) and indirect. Men are more deflective while women are more deceptive. Men are honest liars – they give themselves alibis; their lies are straightforward, simple even; women's are more contorted, convoluted and clever.

Women lie with their lip line. Men lie with their wallets. Women lie about their age and their orgasms just as men lie about their money and their members. Men lie about their earnings and their height. Women lie about their age and their weight. Both sexes lie about the number of sexual partners they have had. Men lie about love ('I love you; of course I do') – they will say anything to get women into bed; women lie about sex ('You were great'; 'Honestly, it isn't a problem'). Women want to be lied to but only in accordance with their desire. Men like to be lied to but in accordance with their egos.

Women lie when they say they would never change anything about you. They also lie about liking your friends. Women lie when they say they like spending time with your family; they lie about it not being a problem when you want to watch soccer on TV or drink with your mates. And if you tell her she looks great in that dress, she'll accuse you of lying! Women lie when they say that they don't mind you looking at other women, or when they say that they don't care about a man's bank account (they seek financial stability and security, so of course they care). Women lie with their bodies in that they can present to men a complete falseness in that they may have fake boobs, fake hair, fake eyelashes, facelifts, and fake orgasms (50 per cent of women lie about having had an orgasm). Women can fake cry in order to emotionally control men. Men are at war with women – they always have been, not to mention with each other.

Men lie when they say to a woman, 'I'll call you'! 'Tell me lies,' as the Fleetwood Mac lyrics go. When women say, 'I just want you to be honest,' they lie. Similarly, when a woman says, 'I'm not angry at you,' she usually is. Because many women have been hurt by men, this phrase is used as an emotional defence. She will pretend she doesn't really care and erect the flimsiest façade to indicate otherwise, followed by the 'silent treatment'.

Women lie in order to make the company around them feel more comfortable. Men lie by trying to create a better image about themselves. The question is: Why do women lie? (Well, why does anybody do anything?). Probably because they don't feel safe. Women also lie for the sake of peace and harmony in the household; they tell their male partners that the handbag they purchased was on sale and they got it at a reduced price ('oh that old thing, I've always had it'; 'they were practically giving it away').

Both men and women lie in approximately a fifth of their social exchanges lasting ten minutes or more. Over the course of a week they deceive about 30 per cent of those with whom they interact. Relationships between parents and teenagers are notorious magnets for deception. College students lie to their mothers in one out of two conversations (excluding mindless pleasantries and polite equivocations such as saying, 'I'm fine, thanks' when they are in fact feeling lousy). Eighty-five per cent of couples in one study reported that one or both partners had lied about past relationships and recent indiscretions. Courting couples lie in about a third of their interactions. Marriage seems to offer some protection against deception: spouses lie to each other in about ten per cent of their major conversations. Eighty-three per cent (in one study) of both men and women said they could tell if their partner was lying. A quarter of women lie about who the father of their child is. Psychological experiments carried out have shown that new acquaintances lie to each other at least three times within the first ten minutes of meeting.

Big lies can become toxic but little lies serve as a harmless social lubricant. There are kind lies: 'Your cakes are the best.' So if you know what's good for you, you'll lie ('you're saying I'm fat so? God, there's no need to be that honest').

Men lie because they see it as 'normal' and unimportant; they lie for the fun of it – being able to lie is felt to be a guarantee of their freedom. Men lie because they think women won't understand. It's based on a fear that she won't see his point of view. Men think that women can't face the truth. Men lie to avoid conflict (lying as an easy option) and confrontation. Men will exaggerate, distort and delete certain truths in the combative world of dating and relationships. Women lie to make others feel better: 'This dinner is simply delicious, a gastronomical delight,' as they gag on every mouthful. By contrast, at the heart of men's lies is the male ego. Men lie to build themselves up, to enhance themselves rather than the Other, as is the case with women. 'Yes, dear, I'll be there in a second,' as he continues to read the newspaper (there's no argument to 'yes'); few things annoy men more than women's 'nagging', so he lies to avoid a scene. Just as few things annoy women more than calling their husbands (or any alternative) by their names and them not responding. I asked earlier, who is better at lying, men or women? We can see from the above analysis that lying is an equal opportunity employer. Perhaps women are better at it, though men get in more practice (four to five times more if statistics are to be believed). Some UK studies have found that men lie twice as much as women with six fibs a day compared to women's three or four, but studies in the US claim we lie on average about 11 times a week. So there are marked discrepancies in the studies.

Men lie upwards. In other words, men pretend they make more money than they actually do, they pretend that they are taller than they actually are and that they have had more sexual partners than they did. Women lie downwards. In other words, women pretend that they are younger than they actually are; they pretend that they are lighter than they actually are and that they have had fewer sexual partners than is the case. Men lie and pretend to be what they will be in the future (or in their fantasy) while women lie and pretend to be what they used to be before in the past.

The top lies men tell: 'I'm fine. Nothing's wrong.' 'Coming dear.' 'I'll have one last pint for the road.' 'I'd no signal.' 'My battery died.' 'I didn't drink too much.' 'I'm on my way now' or 'I'll be there in a second.' 'I'm stuck in traffic.' 'The cheque's in the post.' 'It will never happen again.' 'It didn't mean anything.' 'I don't fancy her.' 'I am paying attention; don't I always?'

The top lies women tell: 'I'm fine. Nothing's wrong.' 'This isn't new – I've had it for years.' 'It wasn't that expensive' or 'I got it in the sales.' 'I'm on my way now.' 'I don't know where they are – I never touched your stuff.' 'I've a headache.' 'I didn't throw it away.' 'We're just friends.' Women think they lie more cleverly than men. Often they do. Women lie about important issues; men lie about more insignificant things.

If lying is bad for your health and stresses the deceiver out physically and psychologically, why do we lie? Men think that lies are not very important, that it's a part of their freedom, as I said earlier; most men lie because they think women won't see their side of the story. They think that by lying things will go on as before but lies grow wings and truth has an uncanny way of getting out. Both sexes lie about their alleged loyalty, especially in matters of love. For few people are fully faithful. Where, dear reader, do your loyalties lie?

The unconscious can answer that. In *The Four Fundamental Concepts of Psycho-Analysis*, Lacan says the following:

• •

'... it is as establishing itself in, and even by, a certain lie, that we set up the dimension of truth, in which respect it is not, strictly speaking, shaken, since the lie as such is itself posited in this dimension of truth.'

• •

In other words, a too formal logic introduces absurdities. For example, to say, 'I am lying' is to tell the truth. 'I am lying' ... about which 'everyone knows there is no such thing'. Lacan explains: 'It is quite wrong to reply to this I am lying – If you say, I am lying, you are telling the truth, and therefore you are not lying, and so on. It is quite clear that the I am lying, despite its paradox, is perfectly valid.'

To say 'I am lying' is not always the declaration of the intention of deceiving; it may operate in the dimension of truth. To say, 'I am deceiving you' is to send out a message in inverted form. It is to say, 'I am telling you the truth'. In the way of deception one is telling the truth. Putting that another way, the (unconscious) truth stumbles in the (conscious) lie.

In summary: Men lie under the pretext of truth. What does this mean? At the level of factual accuracy, men's statements are true, as a rule. Men use factual accuracy to dissimulate the truth about their desire. Žižek gives this example: when my enemy has a car accident due to a brake malfunction, men go to great lengths to explain to everyone that they were never near his car and aren't responsible for the brake malfunction. While this is true, this 'truth' is propagated in order to conceal the fact that the accident realised their desire. By contrast, women tell the truth in the guise of a lie; the truth of women's desire articulates itself in the very distortions of the factual accuracy of her speech. Women's lies unknowingly articulate the truth about their desire; there is a difference, more so for women than men, between factual truth and subjective truth. For women, all truth is subjective.

Lacan once said: 'I, truth, will speak.' The truth will out when the Other of the unconscious speaks, since what it says is not nothing. The unconscious speaks at the margins of meaning – in puns, allusions, jokes, lapsus, logical contradictions, and language games. In all these, glimpses of the truth emerge. We see the world through language. Take this example: 'This is not a pipe' ('*Ceci n'est pas une pipe*').

The words were written by René Magritte under his painting of a pipe. (The camera always lies and mirrors too). But it looks like a pipe. So why isn't it a pipe? Well, because it's a painting. The truth of the unconscious reveals itself through errors and lies. These, then, are our truth.

Cultural Lies

I cited a French painter above. There are cultural lies: the Irish, because we are storytellers and perhaps due to the English colonisation of us as a race, have a peculiar relationship to the truth. We Irish are more circuitous, more circumlocutious with our language which makes truth-telling more problematic. We love to exaggerate and embellish. Of course the laws of libel and slander in each country ensure that this doesn't go too far; after all, some people's reputations may be at stake.

The lies of childhood catch up on us all. They make us creative. It was Karl Popper, the British philosopher, who equated the capacity to lie with the ability to imagine. We have seen how Kant forbade all lying (except to children); if one lies one denies one's right to one's own truthfulness. David Hume, by contrast, understood much better that we all need to lie culturally, sociologically, just to get through the day; he pragmatically permitted the lie in order to allow for smooth social functioning. Few philosophers were prepared to go all the way with Voltaire who, in 1736, wrote:

• •

**'A lie is a vice only when it does harm; it is a
very great virtue when it does good.
So, be more virtuous than ever. You must
lie like a devil, not timidly, but for a while,
but boldly, and persistently ... Lie,
my friends, lie, I shall repay you
when I get the chance.'**

• • • • • • • • • • • • • • • • • •

(This is reminiscent of Martin Luther's injunction to sin boldly). To the question: what if everyone were to lie? Groucho Marx responds: 'Then I'd be a fool not to!' It is the lie more than the laugh that is constitutive of man. Lying is as old as language. As humans we have been brought up to know the etiquette of this particular language game and to be able to distinguish between white lies and lovers' lies. The question is: is there such a thing as the 'perfect lie'? Proust has this to say in volume three of *Remembrance of Things Past*:

• •

**'The lie, the perfect lie, about people we
know, about the relations we have had with
them, about our motive for some action,
formulated in totally different terms, the lie
as to what we are, whom we love, what we
feel with regard to people who love us and**

believe that they have fashioned us in their
own image because they keep on kissing
us morning, noon and night – that lie is one
of the few things in the world that can open
windows for us on to what is new
and unknown, that can awaken in us
sleeping senses for the contemplation
of universes that otherwise we should
have never known.'

• • • • • • • • • • • • • • • •

In short, our lies bespeak our truth.

The Unconscious

Throughout this book I have frequently mentioned 'the unconscious'. However, in a sense 'the unconscious' doesn't exist. Rather, to be more precise, there are unconscious mental processes. 'The unconscious' is best considered in terms of an event rather than an entity, as an adjective rather than a substantive noun. I want to end this book just as I began it, with a definition, perhaps more of a description, of 'the unconscious', by distinguishing four terms. These are:

1: Known knowns (things we know that we know)

2: Known unknowns (things we know we don't know)

3: Unknown unknowns (things we don't know we don't know)

4: Unknown knowns (things we don't know we know).

This fourth one is the (Freudian) unconscious. It is best brought out by way of a story concerning a worker (in some versions he is a prisoner) who was suspected of stealing. Every evening, when he was leaving the factory, the wheelbarrow which he was pushing in front of him was carefully inspected but was always found to be empty until, finally, the guards realised that the worker was stealing the wheelbarrows themselves! Now the unconscious is not what's in the wheelbarrow; it's the wheelbarrow itself. The unconscious is an unknown knowledge. That's the truth of it. The unconscious never lies.

Postscript

This book has attempted to answer the question as to how men and women lie in different ways and to adduce why this is the case, though I spent more time on an analysis of the former than the latter. We have seen that there are different types of lies and that hardly a single day goes by in which we don't lie for whatever reason: to bolster our fragile egos, to compensate for an imagined or real hurt or damage done to our prestige or sense of self, to make the other person feel good or better about themselves, to hurt and harm the other, out of maliciousness or melodrama, from wanton cruelty or ethical kindness, to pass the time or simply for the sheer fun of it.

Pascal, the French philosopher, had said that the heart has its reasons of which reason knows nothing. We don't know what battles are waged in the heart of men and women, what refrains and rages, what resentments and reactions, what regrets and reticence, what remorse and what rebukes. Nobody knows what lies within – no philosopher and no theologian, no psychoanalyst and no anthropologist. We are mysteries to ourselves and don't know why we do what we do most of the time. This is as it should be. Perhaps at the end things may be explained to us and not just interpreted by us.

In the dark heart of men and women there lies also grace and glimmers of something more shining through, something holy, something numinous and luminous that enkindles a light in our midst; it may lead the way; it could be called 'conscience'. We may lie a lot but we mortals are moral too; we are creatures of clay and dust and so we shouldn't be too hard on ourselves for our little lies and yet we should also strive for more, so much more and certainly try to avoid the big Lie.

Evil may be alluring but the Good is magnetic; it draws us still. Evil is radical and all around us ('see how the wicked prosper') but the Good is originary ('God saw that it was good'). It attracts us through love rather than lies. Love is the real lie of the land. Love and Reason are the twin pillars of reality, as the endless battle between God (Truth as a Person) and Satan (the Father of Lies) is being played out in the drama that is life. Socrates said that the worst thing a man can do is to lie in his soul about the Good. This just about sums it all up. For me, at any rate.

Select Bibliography

Augustine, St. 'De Mendacio (Lying) and Contra Mendacio (Against Lying)' in R. J. Deferrari, ed., *Treatises on Various Subjects*. Catholic University of America Press: New York, 1952.

Bacon, Francis. 'Of Truth', *Essays*. Wordsworth Classics of World Literature: Hertfordshire, 1997.

Barnes, Julian. *A History of the World in 10½ Chapters*. Cambridge University Press: Cambridge, 1996.

Campbell, Jeremy. *The Liar's Tale*. W.W. Norton and Company: New York and London, 2001.

Forrester, John. *Truth Games: Lies, Money, and Psychoanalysis*. Harvard University Press: Cambridge, Massachusetts and London, England, 1997.

Frankl, Viktor. *The Doctor and the Soul*. Souvenir Press: London, 2009 (1969).

Freud, Sigmund. 'Two Lies Told by Children'. *The Standard Edition of the Complete Psychological Works of Sigmund Freud*, 1913, vol. 12.

Freud, Sigmund. 'The Psychogenesis of a Case of Homosexuality in a Woman'. *The Standard Edition of the Complete Psychological Works of Sigmund Freud*, 1920, vol. 18.

Freud, Sigmund. 'The Future of an Illusion'. *The Standard Edition of the Complete Psychological Works of Sigmund Freud*, 1927, vol. 21.

Select Bibliography

Freud, Sigmund. 'Jokes and Their Relation to an Unconscious'. The *Standard Edition of the Complete Psychological Works of Sigmund Freud*, 1905, vol. 8.

Hume, David. *An Enquiry Concerning Human Understanding*. Clarendon Press: Oxford, 1975.

Kant, Immanuel. 'On a Supposed Right to Tell Lies from Benevolent Motives' (1797), *Critique of Practical Reason and Other Writings in Moral Philosophy*. Ed., Lewis White Beck. Chicago University Press: Chicago, 1949.

Lacan, Jacques. *The Four Fundamental Concepts of Psycho-Analysis*. Penguin Books: London, 1977.

Montaigne, Michel de. 'On Giving the Lie', *The Complete Essays*. Penguin Books: London, 1991.

Nietzsche, Friedrich. 'Knowledge: Theoretical Introduction on Truth and Lies in an Extra-Moral Sense and On Truth and Lies', in *Philosophy and Truth: Selections from Nietzsche's Notebooks of the Early 1870's*. Ed., Daniel Breazeale. Humanities: New York, 1979.

Sartre, Jean-Paul. *Being and Nothingness: A Phenomenological Essay on Ontology*. (1943). Philosophical Library: New York, 1956.

Sartre, Jean-Paul. *A Sketch for a Theory of the Emotions*. Routledge: London and New York, 1994.

Wilde, Oscar. 'The Decay of Lying', *The Complete Works of Oscar Wilde*. Hamlyn: London-New York-Sydney-Toronto, 1986 (1963).

Wilde, Oscar. 'The Truth of Masks', *The Complete Works of Oscar Wilde*. Hamlyn: London-New York-Sydney-Toronto, 1986 (1963).

Wilde, Oscar. 'De Profundis', *The Complete Works of Oscar Wilde*. Hamlyn: London-New York-Sydney-Toronto, 1986 (1963).

Wittgenstein, Ludwig. *Culture and Value*. Blackwell Publishing: London, 2002 (1977).

Wittgenstein, Ludwig. *Remarks on the Foundations of Mathematics*. Blackwell: London, 1978.

Žižek, Slavoj. *The Puppet and the Dwarf: The Perverse Core of Christianity*. The MIT Press: Cambridge, Massachusetts and London, England, 2003.

Žižek, Slavoj. *The Fragile Absolute*. Verso: London and New York, 2000.

Index